"Since children don't come with checklists or users' manuals, this book will certainly come in handy!"

Roland Warren
President of National Fatherhood Initiative

"Joe Deyo has created the playbook for fatherhood—written for the way men think. *Checklists* will empower new dads to step up to the plate."

David J. White, M.D.

"Moms will love how this book encourages new fathers to take an active role in their families. It gets men involved and helping in all aspects of pregnancy, delivery, and life at home with children."

Kathleen Flowers
Wife and mother of three

"This book offers great wisdom and insight that can really make a difference in the life of your child—and your wife will appreciate it too."

Mike Singletary
NFL Coach and Hall of Fame Member

"Joe Deyo's 5 P's and to-the-point checklists will help even the busiest dads connect . . . in a meaningful way."

Armin Brott
Author of *The Expectant Father* and
The New Father: A Dad's Guide to the First Year

Checklists
for the New Dad

The Expectant Father's Guide
to Pregnancy, Delivery, and Baby's First Year

BY JOE DEYO

SAWTOOTH
PUBLISHING

Spring Hill, Tennessee

ISBN: 978-0-9815779-4-4

Published by Sawtooth Publishing,
Spring Hill, Tennessee

Library of Congress Control Number: 2008908798

Printed in the United States of America

1 2 3 4 5 6 7 8 9 10   13 12 11 10 09

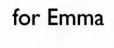

for Emma

Contents

Chapter 8: The First Year / 141

Being a good wagon scout • Baby proofing your home • Toy safety
• Protecting your mate • Baby blues and postpartum depression
• The most important to-do list ever • More baby stuff • First
year dollars and sense • Keeping the love boat afloat • Leading
in the jungle • Baby playtime • Sharpening your father game •
Final marching orders • Chapter Prayer • Wisdom to Consider •
Chapter Checklist

How-To Power Modules / 165

Sources / 203

Glossary / 205

Notes Pages / 233

Index / 245

A Letter from the New Mom
to the New Dad

Dear Dad

Hi. I know it has been crazy for both of us lately, but I want to take just a minute to share a few things I have been thinking about. Please take some time out to listen and then you can be back on your way. I know you have a lot to do because you are a father now. And I am a mother, the mother of your child.

Ever since I was a little girl I have dreamed of being in a fairy tale. My dream always has my wonderful Prince Charming, a man who is strong, courageous, loving, and faithful; my dragon slayer. And after kissing several of life's frogs I finally found my real-life Prince Charming. You! Yes, you. I have chosen you to live out my dream with.

I need you more than ever now. This baby project is going to take everything we both can offer, physically and mentally. Know that I will be giving this everything I have. Also know that when I see the commitment and investment you are putting into our family it makes

**By
Jodie M. Deyo**

my love for you grow even stronger. You are going to do such a great job. This part of our lives will go by fast so let's have fun together and make memories that will last a lifetime.

In my dream there is also a wonderful castle with a moat, towers, and a beautiful grandness. The castle is the home we share together. This part of my dream has also come true! While our home might not have the moat or towers, I think it is plenty grand. You see what I have learned about grand castles is that it doesn't matter what the outside looks like, or the carriage parked in front, or what the furniture looks like on the inside. What makes a castle grand is the love and family found there. And our castle rocks!

Know that I am already very proud of our rocking castle and our growing family. To keep it all running smoothly I am going to need even more of your help. I will need you to do things you may not have done before or that aren't your favorite. There will be lots of dirty diapers and dirty dishes to take care of in our growing family. I need you to help me see what needs done, and I need you to help get it done. And if you can't see what needs done, please ask. We will need plenty of volunteers! Remember I may not always ask you for help so please ask me how you can help. I love options. I will say, "That would be great if you could do that," or I will say, "Thanks for asking, but I can get it this time."

The final piece of my fairy-tale dream is a baby. I have thought about babies for much of my life. As a little girl I played with dolls. As a teenager I would baby-sit. My body reminds me regularly that I am designed for this. I want this baby and I want to be a mom. But know it is not just a baby or motherhood I seek. My ultimate desire is to share the experience of having a child and raising him or her with the man I love. That's really it. We both know this baby is a special gift from God and He wants us to take great care and do the best job we can. Together.

Someone once said that having a baby is like setting a bomb off inside your marriage. Bombs can either destroy what they come in contact with or just rattle the windows a little bit. While I am sure our windows will rattle sometimes, I know this baby is ultimately going to make each of us stronger and strengthen our marriage. After this we will be able to handle whatever blasts come our way in life.

So my Prince Charming, here we are about to give our name to another human being. Let's make it count for something. Let's pour our hearts into it. Let's be great parents. Let's have a great marriage. And let's both know that dreams really do come true.

The Mother of Your Child

Chapter 1

So You Are Going to Be a Father

Even solid marriages can be rocked by a little bundle of joy. Take, for example, my good friend Dave. We have been friends for years and have been through a lot together. Dave's world recently changed a lot. After years of looking for Mrs. Right in all the wrong places he finally found and married a wonderful woman with a great career. They moved to a new house in a different part of town and Dave made a job change. Things have been rolling along pretty well for good ol' Dave.

Before that Dave lived the single life for years. In fact it seemed he kept reliving the same year we all got out of school. He was having a great time while the rest of us were getting pulled into life's natural obligations. Dave didn't worry much about money other than what he had in his pocket at the moment. He had some pretty cool toys that made the guys drool, myself included. Most of the time though he couldn't tell you who his health insurance company was or whether he even had health insurance. His cars were less than practical and his physical and spiritual health would win him no awards. The farthest Dave could see into his future was the next weekend.

Getting married changed Dave some but not a lot. He is still the same carefree and sometimes irresponsible guy. He drives his new wife crazy. But the good news is they love each other to pieces. So much so they decided to move their togetherness to the "next level." They decided it was time to have a baby. It would be so fun!

Lots of their friends had babies. They would have someone to take pictures of with their cool new digital camera. They would have someone to take care of them in their later years. And then the big one came.

The key to surviving it all and emerging with a healthy family and even stronger marriage is turning good information into good action.

The big one was Dave's startling wake-up call. He accomplished one of the easiest parts of fatherhood: conception. He felt great about this contribution, but now what was he supposed to do? His wife was reading thick books and magazines on pregnancy, delivery, and parenting. She was excited, talking with her friends about every aspect of it as easily as a discussion of the weather or last night's ball game. Dave was beginning to have lots of thoughts too.

At the top of his list were questions such as *what do I do now? What is my role? Am I not a 50 percent owner of this little project too? What am I supposed to say to my wife? How can I help my wife? Should I boil some water like they did in the old movies when a baby was about to be born?*

Other pressing questions and concerns started to surface. For example, Dave's wife mentioned once that when they had children she would love to have the option to leave her job and stay at home. *Say what?* Dave was wondering how they would survive financially without her income. What about the awesome benefits her work provided? What about their house? It needed some work, but he was planning on renovating it himself over the next few years and eventually selling it to make a good profit. What about his car? His wife hated to drive it because she didn't feel safe. What about his toys? What about his friends? What about his free time? Who was going to make his dinner?

Along with these burning questions, Dave was also wrestling with the whole "I don't know how to be a good dad" thing. His own father was not a great role model and was not really there for Dave and his mom. Dave wanted to do a better job, but how? It was obvious the big one had a strangle hold on my friend Dave.

So What Is a Guy to Do?

The good news is Dave is not alone as he takes the stage in his new role as a father. More than 4 million babies are born each year in the United States alone. Forty percent of these little ones are coming home to first-time parents.[1] There are a lot of men going through a lot of changes every year.

You may be able to relate to some of Dave's situation, or maybe you have a friend you observed go through some of the same struggle. Many men wrestle with adapting to this season of life. It really is a whole new ball game. And if you don't get a handle on it and understand what is happening it can cause huge stress on a marriage.

So how do you, Dave, and all of the other dads out there make this a winning season of life? The key to surviving it all and emerging with a healthy family and even stronger marriage is *turning good information into good action.* Help is on the way in these pages. This book will give you information, ideas, and "to do's" that will help you become the great father and husband you want to be. A simple model will be outlined to help you put your thoughts and actions to good use. You will find your role, figure out the finances, learn how to change a diaper, know what to say and do, and everything in between.

In addition to a checklist you will find two other resources at the end of each chapter to help get your Dad juices flowing.

"Wisdom to Consider" comes from a variety of sources and helps hammer home the point in just a few words. The "Chapter Prayer" helps you focus on your father role and ask for the power to get it done. Even the world-famous twelve-step programs, which have helped millions of people gain control of their lives, use a standard prayer. As you move into the father phase of life these prayers will help strengthen and guide your journey as well.

But before you get started a little reflection is necessary. The first thing you need to understand is why God has blessed you with this experience (having children) and why you, Dad, are such an important part of the whole plan.

Fathers You Have Known

Any discussion of you as a father would be incomplete without settling up with your past and putting it into your own context. Think about your father. Many of today's new fathers have grown up without their biological father or any father figure physically in the home. Maybe your father was physically present but was absent emotionally and didn't give you the support and guidance you needed. Or maybe you had an awesome dad and loved almost every minute you were together. Maybe your experience with your dad is somewhere in between.

Think about what you liked and didn't like. What do you want to apply to your own blueprint for fathering? Your answer might be none, some, or a lot. Whatever your answer, know you have a clean slate on which to write your script as a father. If your father made big mistakes, vow not to repeat them. If he instilled some things you like, plan to carry them on.

Do the same evaluation of other fathers and father figures you have observed throughout your life. They could be your friends' dads, a close family member, a sports coach, or friends and coworkers. What do you like about their fathering style? What don't you like? What kind of dad do you want to be? What kind of husband do you want to be?

Whatever your bundle of dad experience is, you have it for a reason. Use that experience to improve your game as you step up to be a father. Think about what you experienced and how you will do things different, or how you will do them the same. If your father left some wounds on you then you need to deal with those and move on. This is a new day.

Sit down and write out some goals or words you want to apply as a father and husband. The Notes section of this book is a great place to start. This exercise is an important first step in building your unique approach to manhood and its many stages. It will be part of a foundation that helps guide you not only through pregnancy and delivery but through your child's entire life.

Changing Times

One thing is for certain: whatever game your dad or other dads you knew as a kid brought probably won't work entirely for you in today's fathering world. Take, for example, the National Football League of twenty or thirty years ago. It was much different than the NFL of today. Sure the fundamentals of blocking, tackling, and catching the ball are the same. But much has changed. Today's athletes are stronger and faster. The speed of the game is quicker. Schemes are more complex. Players and coaches have to make more decisions, reads, and changes faster than ever before. The same holds true for fathering today.

So just like my old friend Dave you are going to have to face the facts; you have to adjust your game and change some things. Most people don't have trouble seeing what they want to be or where they want to go in life. For most, the goals as a father are fairly clear. The part people have a hard time with is what they are going to give up or change to get where they want to go.

I can give you two examples of the changes that came around for me. When my wife and I found out we were going to have our first baby we quickly realized we would need some cash to fund the whole adventure. It wasn't long before my favorite guy toy went into the want ads—my jet ski. It was a definite holdover from my bachelor days. Another thing out the door was about one hour of sleep per day. Something had to give in order to get my regular tasks done each day and new tasks before and after the baby arrived. For me it meant I had to get up an hour earlier each day. Sorry, dude—no more sleeping in.

So what will you change to be the dad you want to be? We aren't talking about an extreme makeover or an estate sale here. But know that some things will have to change. Accept this principle and plant it firmly in your mind as we will return to it often. It is the key to releasing the super dad and super husband you want to be.

Children as a Chisel

So what else can you expect out of this whole baby project? Remember, God is always improving you and often uses children to do it. Having children has taught me some of the best lessons of my life. As a father you will learn new skills you haven't possessed before. You will think differently and act differently. You will grow like you never thought possible.

There is one key to unleashing the personal growth children bring. That key my friend is a *successful marriage and relationship with your partner*. Without this you are going to have a very tough time and so will your spouse and children.

Here is the straight scoop on kids: they are a tremendous blessing but they are a lot of work physically, emotionally, mentally, and spiritually. That work makes you tired and leads to stress. You and your wife will be taken to your physical and mental limits regularly with children, from pregnancy through their adult lives. Your marriage has to be in tiptop condition to handle this load and the strain it creates.

As a father you will learn new skills you haven't possessed before. . . . You will grow like you never thought possible.

Think of your marriage as the engine of a car. The rest of your life including children is the rest of the car—the transmission, the wheels, the body, and everything else. You can pour as much time, thought, and money into these other parts of your life as you want, including children. But if the engine is out of tune the whole car will suffer and you won't go anywhere. And we all know a broken car is frustrating and no fun.

Your marriage engine must be tuned and made a priority. If it's running strong and dependably it's a piece of cake to work on all of the other pieces of your life's car. So keep it in tune. Work on it. Let change happen in a positive way. Just like the list of goals you are putting together for your role as father, spend just as much thought on what kind of husband you want to be in this season of life.

The 5 P's

There is a way to help bring clarity to all of this super dad and super husband talk. A simple model was mentioned earlier that will help organize your goals and actions as husband and father. It is called the 5 P's and we will refer to it often. The 5 P's are: be present, protect, provide, partner, and play. Let's set the stage for each of these.

1. Be Present

As a father you must be present physically and mentally in every way for your family. It isn't all about you anymore. Actually, it never was. It's about you and your wife enjoying a great marriage and raising a healthy and happy human being. There are lots of eye-opening stats if you were wondering what stake you as a fully present father have in this whole thing. Consider these sample study results published by the National Fatherhood Initiative in the book *Father Facts*[2]:

→ Compared to living with both parents, living in a single-parent home doubles the risk a child will suffer from physical, emotional, or educational neglect.

→ Children living with both parents do better in school than children in all other family types.

→ Children living in a two-parent household with a poor relationship with their father are 68 percent more likely to smoke, drink, or use drugs compared to all teens in two-parent households.

→ Boys who grow up outside of intact marriages are more than twice as likely as other boys to end up in jail.

→ 76 percent of teenage girls say their fathers are very or somewhat influential on their decision to have sex.

→ 90 percent of homeless children come from fatherless homes.

→ Children from single-mother families are one and a half to two times more likely to have one or more behavioral or emotional problems compared to those living in two-parent married households.

→ Children in father-absent homes are five times more likely to be poor.

→ Those who experience parental divorce or separation as children tend to average a shorter life span by more than four years.

These stats show a rough road for many kids growing up in homes where dads are physically absent. Just as sobering is the damage done to children and marriages by men who are mentally, emotionally, or spiritually absent in the home. It won't work out well if you expect to sit in a recliner at the end of the day and grunt a couple of times at your wife and children. It's wrong to expect your wife to handle it all from diapers through diplomas. Consider the results of a national survey also published in *Father Facts:* a resounding 96 percent of respondents agreed that parents should share equally in the care taking of children.

Sorry, dude, the 1950s are over. You're all in. Your role as a father can't be taken lightly. You must be present—physically, emotionally, mentally, and spiritually—to do the best possible job. Embrace the importance of fatherhood early on and make an unbreakable commitment to see it through in person.

2. Protect

There is no way to set a value on your mate. You must view her as the most precious person in the world. One of your big assignments as a man is to nurture and protect that person. When we talk about protecting we usually think first of physical protection; keeping a roof over our family and fighting off the bad guys who try to break in. Of course these are priorities and need to be part of your plan. Most guys instinctively know how to get these things done.

But to be the super husband/dad you will want to expand the definition of physical protection. During pregnancy this is especially true. Your wife won't be able to do as much physically as she used to. There will be times when she has less energy, less mobility, less everything. This is when you need to help her by stepping up your protection level. Carry in the groceries, clean the house, run some errands, paint the nursery, massage her back, milk the cows, and hoe the corn. You will need to coach (and restrain) her on some other things as well. My wife, for example, loves to decorate. While very pregnant with our second child I caught her hanging off the top step of a ladder trying to finish some painting. "Honey, that is a no-no."

The other phase of protection, as important as the physical part, is mental protection. Just as your wife's body will be pushed to its physical design limits, so will her mind. Moms face an incredible learning curve with a mountain of information to consume. Her emotions are larger than ever and are fueled by a huge supply of hormone gasoline. And she is having a baby, one of the most exciting and challenging events of her life. Her mind has a lot to handle. Combine this with her physical situation and you see why her plate is full.

So, how can a bunch of hairy-legged boys like us help in such a situation? The key is to help her carry the mental and emotional load. Just like the physical part of carrying in the groceries you can do much the same in the mental arena. One example might be serving as her "scribe" at her regular doctor visits. Write her questions down before you go in and write down the information the doctor gives. Hold her hand and offer support. While this one example in itself doesn't seem like much, combining it with several other similar things will help take the edge off her mental strain and help her stay more relaxed.

Through the next few chapters we will discuss in detail how to "get in the game" and make sure you are doing everything you can to protect your wife physically and mentally. During pregnancy, delivery, and the years beyond, your protection P needs to be at the top of its game. Not only are you protecting your wife but you are also protecting your child. It is a great assignment.

3. Provide

A man's role as provider is pretty clear even in today's home where it is often shared. The Bible states in 1 Timothy 5:8, "If anyone does not provide for his relatives, and especially for his immediate family, he has denied the faith and is worse than an unbeliever." All righty then. That is clear. But what does providing really mean in today's times?

Just a generation or two ago providing encompassed paying the rent or mortgage and putting food on the table. You went to work and brought home a paycheck. If you did that you received an *A*. Your own father may have even seen this as his main task in the family. A home and food on the table certainly remain as your responsibility today, and it is squarely on your shoulders to make sure these basics are covered.

By giving your wife unconditional love you will give her the ultimate security.

In later chapters we will take the food and home concept to the next level. In a nutshell it still comes down to earning a steady income. But there are also other things you need to have, such as disability insurance and life insurance, should your ability to earn an income slow down or stop.

Beyond the home and food the providing duties of today's husbands and fathers are more involved. These are best categorized by a couple of "L" words: love and leadership. The importance of each can't be underestimated.

By giving your wife unconditional love (think real love here not just sex) you will give her the ultimate security. Security breeds confidence and confidence breeds energy and enthusiasm, two key ingredients for a super wife and a super mom. Providing your mate unconditional love is powerful stuff!

Leadership is the other thing you need to work on providing. It isn't the army general kind of leadership you might think of, though you are encouraged to use that style if necessary in the delivery room. The brand of leadership you need to display is leading by example. Jumping in and doing the household chores when everyone is out of gas. Getting up early and staying up late to get things done. Offering encouraging words. Changing a diaper when it's not your turn. Bringing up the tough topics. Looking into the future. All of these are examples of the leadership you need to provide.

4. Partner

The fourth of the 5 P's is partnering. It can be the most difficult for many men. Bringing a new baby into the world requires a new level of working together for the couple. And, oh my goodness, it will require some of the *C* word from the man; it will require some *change*.

Partnering is a key theme you will find throughout this book, but what exactly does partnering mean? True partnering is working with your spouse to handle all the to-do's that come along with pregnancy and raising a baby. These to-do's aren't just physical ones like cleaning the house. There are mental and spiritual to-do's to work on together. They can be the fun ones like picking out the name of your child. Or they can be not so fun ones like naming a guardian to raise your children should you both die. You will need to work as a team more than ever.

5. Let's Play!

The fifth and final *P* is play. This is the fun one! You know bringing a child into the world is a serious endeavor and a lot of hard work. To make it all work you will need a good sense of humor and a desire to have fun along the way. You need to play!

Smiling and laughter have long been proven as wonderful medicines. This is medicine your marriage and your children will need from you in the years ahead. So loosen up and don't take yourself so seriously all the time. Laugh at your mistakes. Savor those baby moments. Hold your wife's hand. Go on a date. Be crazy in love with your family and show it to the world!

What playing like a grown-up is not is humor at the expense of others for your own fun. So, no practical jokes, big guy. Those aimed at your wife will be especially unappreciated during these times. In addition to good humor, always be on the lookout for simply fun things for you and your family to do.

Good play is critical in navigating the choppy waters of pregnancy, delivery, and your baby's first year. The humor and sense of fun you use now will also serve you well in the years ahead. This book will give you some ideas for play to help strengthen your marriage, your relationship with your children, and your own life.

Jump In and Swim

There is no room for me, me, and me in the world of baby. Just like the best pro sports teams you can't have one person who isn't working for the good of the entire group. If you do, it is a distraction and saps all of the energy from the team. The information and checklists presented in this book will help drive you to a more solid and rewarding partnership with your spouse. And it will put you on the path to being the super dad you were designed to be. So take a deep breath and dive into this new phase of life. The water is awesome.

DEAR FATHER, thank You for blessing me with the opportunity to be a father. Bless my mind, heart, and hands with the ability to be a great one. Bless my wife and our marriage as we open this new chapter of life. Help me be present, to protect, provide, partner, and play. Guide me in leadership and love. Bless this growing family and hold us in the palm of Your hand. In the name of the Father of all fathers I pray, **AMEN.**

Wisdom to Consider

"Husbands, love your wives,
just as Christ loved the church
and gave himself up for her."
EPHESIANS 5:25

As you take the journey of bringing a child into the world, loving your wife needs to be at the top of your list. Absorbing this material and working through the checklist items is a great place to start.

☑ CHAPTER CHECKLIST

❏ Tell your wife you love her every day. Tell her at least every week you are excited to be having a baby with her.

❏ Tell your wife you want to be a super husband and a super father and you are going to be working hard to do so.

❏ Make a list of goals on what you want to do as a husband during pregnancy. Then move on doing them.

❏ Work hard on your marriage. Plan some dates, write your wife a card every so often, leave her a note, open the car door for her, and perform some other small acts of kindness for her.

❏ If you aren't already, begin to pray at least once a day with your wife. Pray for your marriage, your home, your new baby, good health, and anything else that needs attention in your life.

❏ Think about your experiences with your own father and other dads you have observed. What did you like and not like?

❏ Make a list of your goals as a dad. What are your priorities? What kind of dad do you want to be? Do the same for your role as a husband. Use the Notes section of this book as a place to start.

❏ Brainstorm a list of things you may have to change in your life to become the father and husband you want to be. This might include spending, work habits, home life, travel, outside activities, personal habits, priorities, and more.

❏ Write a letter to your unborn child. Include your thoughts, your hopes, and your promise to be the best father you can be. Make it fun and personal. Let your wife read it then stow it away for your child as a keepsake.

❑ Think regularly about the 5 P's of being present, protecting, providing, partnering, and playing. How can you do more of each of these every day?

❑ Work on providing love and leadership in your home.

❑ Enjoy this time! Laugh and dream with your wife. Drink in the moments and remember this as one of the best times of your life. There are more to come.

Chapter 2

Getting Your Head in the Game

▶ If you have participated in sports or watched sports you are probably familiar with this situation. It involves a team working hard to win and a coach who is passionate about the game.

Each player brings his own strengths and contributions to the team. But there comes a time when a player is just not clicking in a game—and he should be. The player is in the arena, he is in uniform and he is in the starting lineup. The team has practiced and has a well thought out strategy to win the game. But our player just isn't doing well. He isn't playing hard or making the right adjustments. At this point you hear our agitated and passionate coach yell from the sideline these famous coaching words: "Get your head in the game!"

So it is with becoming a father. Just because you have the uniform—the ring and the marriage certificate—and just because you are physically in the game—the fun conception part—doesn't automatically mean your head is in the game. Getting your head in the game means *thinking about what to do short term and long term and then moving those thoughts into action.* It is making sure you have all of your bases covered, that you are making the right adjustments and adapting to the game at hand. It is playing with all of your heart.

Getting your head in the game is never more important than during pregnancy. Let's see how we can apply some of our 5 P's even further during these crucial months.

Protect Me

You already know it's your job to protect your wife every day, especially during these nine months of pregnancy. The next chapter highlights the physical things you can do to get your hands in the game and help protect. Here the focus is on the important mental aspects of the game. You will need to sit down with your wife and have a talk about how you can help her in this area. But first let's explore the why and how of this mental protection.

Why is mentally protecting your cherished wife so important? Because, my friend, you should want to reduce as much as possible the STRESS she feels during pregnancy. Stress during pregnancy can come from a number of places, including concern for the child's health, absorbing truckloads of information, and maintaining other life duties just to name a few. *Note:* I said we want to reduce stress not eliminate it, which is impossible during these times.

So why reduce stress? Science clearly proves the mental state is directly chained to the physical state. And you want the best physical state for your pregnant wife so she can deliver a full-term baby after forty weeks. So that means your wife needs a healthy and rested mind to get there.

A mentally overloaded expectant mother can create a burden on her body. In extreme cases that can lead to unwanted health conditions for her and the baby. The number one cause of infant mortality in the United States is premature birth. Premature babies bring a host of challenges and some can't be overcome. Many premature births are due to circumstances out of your control. But as a couple your goal is to focus on what you can control. You want to do everything in your power to get your baby to the full term finish line. One way to help accomplish this is to lighten the mental load of your wife and help create an enjoyable experience. Talk it over and see where you might be able to help out.

Hiring a Manager

One idea you might want to consider is temporarily becoming your wife's manager or gatekeeper for certain people or obligations. Many people in business still use a gatekeeper or receptionist to help screen calls and situations. The goal is to keep the business executive doing what is most important and not caught up in unproductive calls, meetings, and work.

My wife and I employed a similar tactic while she was pregnant. We made a short list of potentially stressful situations and people she wanted me to handle. *Note:* the key words are *she wanted me to handle*. Don't go there if your wife isn't totally on board.

One person in our lives is an excellent example. Let's call her Crisis. Whenever Crisis had a problem or decision to make she would turn to my wife and me for help. And lots of it. It seemed Crisis always had a crisis and she always needed our help. So my wife and I would spend a lot of time working on this friend's problems. Until pregnancy.

You see I grew up in a family of lumberjacks in rural Idaho. The timber business is tough work for tough men. You can't cry if you get a splinter in your finger or even if you break your finger. You have to get the work done without getting hurt or going broke. You have to be logical.

So enter the logical lumberjack gatekeeper for Crisis. When the first issue came up, together we reminded Crisis that Jodie was pregnant. The next nine months were all about Jodie staying healthy and rested, physically and mentally. For various reasons we still felt the need to be involved to some degree with Crisis and her walk through life. But as stated earlier, it isn't about you (Crisis) anymore; it's ALL about a healthy mom and a healthy baby.

If Crisis needed any help with problems or decisions it would be me, the logical lumberjack who would provide it from our family. I would still consult Jodie if necessary but I was serving as the point guard. It worked fabulously for all involved. Crisis emerged as a better decision maker, I learned some new lessons in patience, and my wife stayed rested. So think about who might be your Crisis people, situations, and obligations. What are your wife's mental stress points? If you and your wife are in agreement, set yourself up as the manager or substitute for these during pregnancy. It is good protection and it might turn out to be a long-term win-win for all.

Partner with Me

Now more than ever you need to talk with your wife. Talking with your wife also means listening to your wife, and you will be wise to do lots of listening. The good news for the logical lumberjacks among us (who often don't have much to say) is there is a lot to talk about during pregnancy. If you haven't done so lately it is a great time to think well into the future, beyond the busy year in front of you. Here are some life topics you might want to explore as a couple:

- →ı Are we living in the city, state, or neighborhood we want to be in?
- →ı Are we pursuing the careers we really want to pursue?
- →ı Are we bringing in the income we need to support a family?

- Is our current house going to work with a child? Two children? More?
- Do we have access to the schools we want our children to attend?
- Are we properly plugged in at church? Are we in the right church?
- Are there other couples we could ask to help mentor us as new parents?
- Do we have the support cast of family and friends around us we need?

Some of these topics are more involved than a conversation over a cup of coffee. Some will require some research and some will require change and hard work. The point is the birth of a baby is one of those times in life where you need to do a thorough life checkup. How are we doing? Where are we going? How are we going to get there? Take some notes about each and develop some action plans. The big point in this exercise is that you are partnering with your wife and talking about things *together*. This is a practice you need to sharpen as you begin raising your family. God wants the best for you. Make sure you are reaching for this potential.

Another set of topics to partner on center around the immediate project at hand: the birth of your child. Here are just a few of the things you will want to discuss with your wife:

- What OB/GYN will she be seeing? Does she like him or her? Does she want to change? Will he or she oversee the delivery?
- What pediatrician should we see?
- Where do we want to deliver the baby? What do we want the "tone" of the delivery to be like?
- Do we have our insurance in order for delivery? What finances will we need to pay for delivery?

→ Do we want to find out the sex of the baby? Why or why not?

→ What names do we like for our baby?

→ What furniture, clothes, and other baby gear do we need? Where will the baby sleep? What do we need to do to get it ready?

It is important for both of you to partner on these and other topics sure to come up. Some conversations will be short and some will be long. Some will be easy and some will be hard. The important thing is to have the conversations. Be a leader and start the discussion. Remember to tell your wife you love her and how excited you are to bring a baby into the world with her. Remember, love leads to security for her, security leads to confidence, and confidence leads to energy and enthusiasm and healthy babies!

Working with Physicians

Some of the items in the baby discussion list center around physicians. You and your wife may have a clear vision of who the lead OB/GYN and pediatrician will be for your family. Or you may be considering using a mid-wife, doula, or family practitioner to fill the roles. If you don't have a clear vision for both of these positions you will want to discuss your options as a couple. Find out who your friends and coworkers are seeing. You may even want to go and interview several. Many people invest more research and time into appliance purchases these days than the selection of important physicians. Do some homework and make the best decisions you can with your spouse.

Your wife will likely be the final decision maker on who she wants to use as an OB/GYN. She was probably seeing an OB/GYN prior to pregnancy, and with a baby on board she may just want to continue seeing that doctor. But be sure to ask her if she likes her doctor. If she isn't thrilled, then encourage her to shop around and talk to several if possible. With our first child my wife visited several practices until she found the physician, office staff, and atmosphere that were a fit for her and her personality. For the birth of our third child she found someone she liked even better and switched. Whatever road you take with an OB/GYN be sure you are both comfortable with it. This physician will be the quarterback as you go through pregnancy and delivery. You will be relying on his or her expertise a lot, especially if you have any special situations.

The wonderful world of pregnancy only happens once per child. You can't download the file and play it later when you have time.

The role you play with OB/GYN appointments during pregnancy is clear and easy: go on EVERY appointment you can. Make it a priority. No excuses. Don't be distracted by other dads who profess they met the doctor for the first time at delivery or they just went on a couple of the "big" appointments. You should be there for all of them if humanly possible. Here is why.

The wonderful world of pregnancy only happens once per child. You can't download the file and play it later when you have time. You need to be there to learn what is going on and to enjoy every second of this awesome experience. Most importantly, you need to be there to support and honor your wife.

Remember the discussion earlier about helping reduce her stress levels? Here is where you can step in and do so. During the OB/GYN appointments you can not only offer support but also serve as the scribe. Write down your and your wife's questions before the appointment, even in the waiting room if you have to. This helps remove this load from your wife. During the appointment write down the answers and any other information that comes along with the visit. You will be the one to write down those baby heartbeat counts, so be ready! In addition to being a great reference during pregnancy, these little notes and records you make are a great keepsake. They may even provide you, your wife, and your child a few good laughs. This book is equipped with a handy Notes section just for that purpose.

So do whatever you need to do with your work and life schedule to be part of these visits. Let your wife know you want to be a part. Try to schedule times that will work for both of you. Participating in these appointments establishes you early on as present, physically and mentally. Good habits start here.

Baby Doc

While the final selection of an OB/GYN may fall mostly to your wife, the selection of a pediatrician should be a joint project. After the birth of your baby your wife will probably be seeing the OB/GYN only once or twice a year. With a pediatrician you will be more of a frequent flyer, sometimes seeing them once or twice a month. Both you and your wife really need to like and trust this doctor.

Again, the choice of which pediatrician may be easy. Or you may need to shop around and visit several. Whatever you do, meet the doctor of your choice before you deliver the baby. You don't want to meet them for the first time in the hospital where you deliver or at the two-week checkup. Here are some things you will want to know about the pediatrician you choose:

- →ı Who is the backup group in case your doctor is unavailable?
- →ı How does he or she handle after-hours emergencies?
- →ı How are nonurgent questions handled? Is a nurse available to answer routine questions?
- →ı What is the doctor's schedule for seeing the baby in the first year?

→ı What is the procedure for seeing you in the hospital?

→ı Does he or she make rounds at the hospital you have chosen for the delivery?

→ı How long has the doctor been practicing?

After your baby arrives there will be a set schedule of follow-up visits with the pediatrician. Assuming no special circumstances this will typically be at two weeks, one month, three months, six months, nine months, and one year of age. And guess what? You need to be there for all of these. Just like the OB/GYN appointments, this is your opportunity to be present for your child and your wife. Two sets of parent ears and eyes are always better than one. Ask questions. Take notes. Scribe. Listen. Laugh. Enjoy.

Hear it one more time: this rodeo only happens once. Go to as many of the OB/GYN and pediatrician appointments as humanly possible and you will be recognized as a great husband and a great father. You will be involved and present and your wife will be the envy of her friends.

Walk with Me

There is another key aspect of getting your head in this game that may require a shift in thinking. It is walking side by side with your wife in lifestyle choices. It is doing as she does. It is sharing some of her discomfort. It is changing and enjoying things together. It is ultimate partnering. Consider the following in your walk: smoking, alcohol consumption, diet, exercise, and spirituality.

If either of you smokes, you both need to quit during pregnancy and hopefully quit for good. Your wife quitting will greatly reduce the chance of complications. You quitting will cut the second-hand smoke she and the baby gets. Most importantly it shows support for her and assures her you are walking together as one.

For obvious health reasons your wife should stop drinking any alcohol during pregnancy. You should join her. Partner. Feel better. Save money. Not drinking might even become a life long habit.

Come alongside your wife and exercise together. Mom, dad, and baby will all be winners.

Your wife will have some constraints on what she can eat and drink. No more oysters on the half shell or twice a day trips to Starbucks. Be a super partner and for fun join in some of her new diet restrictions. It will be another great example that you are serious about walking with her.

If your wife exercised regularly before pregnancy she will likely continue with her doctor's approval. If she wasn't exercising routinely she may want to start some activity with her doctor's direction. Whatever the case you should join her as often as you can. A perfect exercise routine for pregnant couples to do together is walking. It is relaxing and while you walk you can talk over some of the topics mentioned earlier. Other exercise options might be swimming, light aerobics, or light weightlifting. Again, talk to your wife's OB/GYN and get approval. Then come alongside your wife and exercise together. Mom, dad, and baby will all be winners.

The most important part of walking together in life and in pregnancy is walking together spiritually. You both need to be working on your relationship with God. You and your wife both need to be plugged in with a church and attending regularly. It won't work if only one of you goes. Walk in together. You also need to pray together. For some couples this is easy and routine. For others it is a little harder. When my own wife and I started to pray together it did feel a little awkward. But today it feels very natural and it is one of the biggest ways we stay connected to each other and to God. If it does feel uncomfortable at first I implore you to push through it. Take that leadership role if you must. Start with simple prayers at the dinner table if you need to. Those couples that pray together every day are truly walking together every day.

Provide Love for Me

You and your wife must have that well-tuned marriage engine as you bring a child into the world. I once heard in a sermon it isn't a house or love that provides children security. It is the commitment children see between their mother and father. Wow. Hopefully your marital relationship is in tip-top shape. Most couples are excited during pregnancy, and you should be as well! Your head and your heart really need to be in this game.

Every now and then many couples could use a refresher course in a key component of marriage: courtship. This word's true meaning often gets lost in today's busy world. It means outwardly demonstrating love for your wife and doing things for her. Think random acts of kindness. Think play. Remember any marriage is the joining of two imperfect people in an imperfect world. Courtship is the grease that helps make all of these clunky gears work.

Try these simple ideas to help in your courtship rebirth:

- → Say, "I love you" at least once a day.
- → Readily say, "I am sorry" and "I forgive you."
- → Always put her first above work, friends, sports, and everything else in your life. Remember, she is the best thing that ever happened to you.
- → Open the car door for your pregnant wife. Make this a lifelong habit.
- → Leave her a hand written note at least once a week.
- → Plan regular dates. I said you plan the date, don't ask her to.
- → Listen; *really listen* to your wife when she talks.

- Surprise her at least monthly with flowers or a small gift. Maybe even a big gift every once in a while.
- Never criticize, correct, or interrupt her in front of others. Playful put-downs are still put-downs—don't go there. Instead, brag on her in front of others.
- Provide lots of extra understanding and slack during pregnancy and the time following. Don't tell her she is acting crazy or not being logical.
- Do all of the checklist items in this book and she will fall in love all over again!

There are all kinds of ways to boost the courtship part of your marriage. Find some more resources or a good book if you need more help. Poll some of your friends and their wives to see what they like to do. The point is you should be fully engaged in this part of your relationship. All work and no play makes for a sluggish marriage engine. You and your wife need to play. Your wife will be excited and secure and return the love. You will benefit as well. Take the lead!

Dad Management

OK, Elvis, by now you are probably all shook up about how you are going to be present and do all of this protecting, providing, partnering, and playing. To do it all you are going to have to be organized and work hard. Along with helping your wife manage herself you are still going to have to manage yourself.

A good place to start is using some basic time management. For example, remember all of those doctor appointments you are going to? These usually get scheduled way in advance so you need to write them down so you don't forget. If you are already using a calendar or scheduling tool, plug them in there. If you don't have a calendar you can always use the Notes section of this book as a starting point. List your appointments, dates with your wife, work-out times, birthdays, anniversary, or other to-do's. Before you go to bed, look at your schedule for the next day. The point is to know the what, when, where, why, and how of your schedule and own it.

Make sure you are using all your available time as wisely as you can. Put some thought into this. Are there any efficiencies you can squeeze out of your day-to-day routine? Can you make phone calls on the way to work? Can you do some of your bill paying on your lunch hour? Can you combine errands? Several excellent books and resources are on the market if you need more of a time management makeover. Take a step back, look at your usual activities, and see what you can improve and make more efficient. You are going to need every extra minute you can find for the next twenty years or so.

Racehorse Care

Just as your pregnant wife is taking extra good care of herself during this time, so should you. You have a lot to handle physically and mentally. I once heard Zig Ziglar, the famous author and motivational speaker, use this analogy regarding the management of your health: If you owned a million dollar racehorse, would you keep him up most of the night before the big race drinking booze, smoking cigarettes, and eating junk food? Good point Zig. You should think of all your days in this phase of life as big race days. So Seattle Slew, off to bed with you. Rest. Exercise. Eat right. Relax. Read. Listen. Think straight. Talk. You have a lot to do and a lot of responsibility. You need to be at the top of your game.

Here is one last word about learning and reading in this special time of life. It is unlikely any one book or information source will fulfill all your unique needs during pregnancy, delivery, and Baby's first year. Every couple has unique needs, challenges, and perspectives during these times. As hard as we try to make this book as complete as possible it may not fulfill all your needs. If your situation requires more information on a topic, ask your doctor, talk to friends, or seek out additional information online or at the bookstore. You need to be a hard working student and learn all you can from the great resources available today. Get your head in the game!

Chapter Prayer

FATHER, let me be alert to the mental and physical needs of my wife during this special time. Grant me the wisdom and energy to help make our home a peaceful and loving place as we prepare for this special baby. Put Your blessing upon the physicians we work with. Help my wife and me walk together in all areas of our lives. Strengthen our marriage. Father, bless my mind and my body. Guide me. In the name of the One who invented love I pray, **AMEN.**

Wisdom to Consider

"By wisdom a house is built, and through understanding it is established; through knowledge its rooms are filled with rare and beautiful treasures."

PROVERBS 24:3–4

Get your head in the game: dream, think, plan, pray, talk, listen, and love. Then go and fill all the rooms of your house with the rare and beautiful treasure of children.

☑ CHAPTER CHECKLIST

❏ Talk with your wife about what might be burdening her mind during this time of pregnancy. Listen and see if there is anything you can do to lighten that load.

❏ Offer to assist your wife as her pregnancy manager / gatekeeper during pregnancy. Are there stressful people or situations she can turn over to you?

❏ Go through the list of "life checkup" questions presented in this chapter. Think hard about such issues as career, lifestyle, home, and location. Are you where you want to be? What changes do you want? Talk it over with your spouse.

❏ Go through the "baby list" questions presented in this chapter. Work closely with your wife on all these and offer support.

❏ Talk with your wife about the selection of an OB/GYN. Does she like the one she has? Encourage her to find one she does like.

❏ Write down all of the OB/GYN appointments and go with your wife to as many as humanly possible.

❏ Talk with your wife about the selection of a pediatrician. Schedule an appointment with that doctor before your baby arrives and go meet him or her.

❏ Remember to serve as official scribe and take notes during all doctor visits. Take this load off your wife's shoulders.

❏ Walk with your wife in lifestyle choices such as eating and exercise. Cut smoking and alcohol out of your lives.

❏ Build a strong spiritual bond with God and with your wife. Pray together. Go to church together.

❑ Practice courtship with your wife. Do the items in the court-ship list in this chapter. Come up with some of your own unique ideas. Show the love!

❑ Manage yourself. Take care of your body and mind. Eat right and get good rest. Get organized. Manage your time and find some extra minutes.

❑ Find the resources and books for areas of your life you want to strengthen. Absorb and apply them.

Chapter 3

Getting Your Hands in the Game

▶ Think back to my friend Dave who just found out his wife is pregnant. One of his big questions and a question of most men whose wives are pregnant is *what should I be doing?* The answer is easy: plenty.

Pregnancy is not a time for you to put your feet up, kick back for nine months, and wait for the timer to go off to get the baby out of the oven. This is the time for you to get up and get your hands in the game. In the last chapter we have covered what you need to be doing mentally. Now we will dig into what you need to be doing physically to ensure your success as a father and husband. Your wife needs you more than ever, so get your butt in gear.

Report for Duty

After you digest this material, the first thing you will want to do is sit down with your wife (again) and talk about how you can help and why you want to. These are new times for her as well and it may add to her stress if you dive into household duties or baby projects she was managing without talking it through first.

Your wife may feel her own challenge to "do it all." She may feel the pull to smoothly handle her own career, manage the house, perform her other life duties, and prepare for the arrival of a child all at the same time. So during your sit down conversation, acknowledge that she is capable of doing it all quite nicely. But then tell her how important it is for you to be involved as well in every phase. You want to build some good habits and routines during pregnancy that will carry on after it gets totally crazy when the baby arrives. Tell her you want her to be able to get some extra rest during pregnancy and you want her to have time to read and prepare. You want to help her carry the load. She will appreciate your support and your willingness to try new things to help.

> *A real man honors his wife by coming alongside her and carrying the load. This is your time, your hour.*

There are a number of ways Super Dad can pitch in and help. For example, each couple is different in how they handle the household tasks of cooking, cleaning, laundry, shopping, paying bills, and running errands. It's great if you are already involved in some or all of these areas. The goal is to not only keep up what you have been doing but also to relieve your wife of some of her routine tasks partially or altogether.

I have seen some men stop cold at the point of jumping in to help. Why? Many are worried they will somehow be surrendering their manhood if they cook dinner, clean a toilet, or write a thank-you note. They think it somehow degrades or diminishes their roar or their style as a man. You need to get over that. A real man honors his wife by coming alongside her and carrying the load. This is your time, your hour. Remember, you are trying to take some of those sharp corners off of your wife's daily load so she is rested and less stressed during this important time of carrying your baby. This is a time for leadership, strength, and taking on new challenges—

all things men are built for. So roll up your sleeves and let's see where you can get your hands in the game.

The Mess Hall

Keeping meals on the table for your wife, yourself, and your growing family can be time consuming. As men, we bring a wide variety of experience into the kitchen. Some men are already regularly preparing meals and cleaning up. Others might not know how to turn on an oven or how to wash dishes. Wherever you are on the scale the good news is this; there is plenty to do at all levels and you are capable of doing it!

While schedules and lifestyles for couples vary, it seems the big meal to handle for most is the evening dinner. Breakfast and lunch are usually easier to handle with cereal, sandwiches, and other grab and go type food. But the evening meal is the traditional time to sit down with a hot plate of food and be together as a family. As your children grow you will want to strive to make the evening dinner a consistent family event that pulls everyone together. Studies show that families who routinely eat together have better communication, better relationships, and better marriages.

Your mission, my good man, is to take responsibility for cooking at least some of these meals. If you are already in this mode, great, keep it up. If this is new ground for you, work with your wife on it. Tell her you want to help and you want to learn some new skills. You want her to take some time off from the kitchen. In our house, for example, I take on the task of preparing dinner two nights a week. I usually accomplish this by preparing a large main course the first night and then we reheat the leftovers the second night. So, one round of cooking covers two meals.

What do you cook, how do you cook, and when do you find time to do it? The key to these questions and achieving success in the kitchen can be found in one word: recipes. These little instruction manuals have been used for centuries to feed the world but are often forgotten by men. A good recipe can be your ticket to stardom. Start looking for these gems and you will see they are everywhere—on soup cans, in newspapers, and even in your mom's head. You may want to pick your wife's brain for her favorites or break new ground on your own. Look at some cookbooks or tap your friends for some of their favorites as well. Keep the following tips in mind as you go:

- Stick with foods both you and your wife enjoy. If she isn't crazy about lamb or salmon, don't try to convert her now.
- Pick recipes with a limited number of ingredients and that consist of things you have at home or you can easily find at the store.
- The kitchen can be frustrating if you don't love being there. Keep your creations tasty but quick and simple to make.
- Pick recipes and dishes that can be built ahead of time and put in the refrigerator before cooking. The first person home can pop it in the oven. Or use a crock-pot you plug in before you head to work in the morning.
- Plan well balanced meals. Remember your wife needs all the right foods now more than ever. Include salads, fruits, vegetables, and whole-wheat bread to round out your main course.
- Have fun and surprise your wife with some awesome dinners.

Time in a Bottle

One of the big challenges in meal prep is finding the time to do it. Depending on your work schedule, it may be impossible to invest an hour in putting dinner together right before it is time to eat. And if you have been working all day you probably aren't in the mood to do it joyfully. I highly recommend you do much of your cooking in off hours, when you first get up in the morning or before you go to bed at night. The refrigerator can be your best friend.

I do some of my best creations at 5:00 in the morning before anyone else in the house is up. Keep in mind these have to be quiet creations; no banging the pots and pans, cursing, or loud chopping is allowed. If your recipes require this, then you may want to prepare them before everyone goes to bed in the evening. Trade in some of your evening remote control time for a mixing spoon and your wife will fall in love all over again.

Trade in some of your evening remote control time for a mixing spoon and your wife will fall in love all over again.

Your goal in all this is to come up with four or five plays in the kitchen you can execute well. Do one a week and make it large enough to cover two nights. Of course you can adjust as necessary to fit your schedules. The most important thing is to make the effort. If you do, your wife will see your hands in the game and appreciate your support.

Clean It

Now that you have a big mess in the kitchen it is time to clean it up. Under no circumstance should you make one of your award winning dinners without putting things away and cleaning up. Washing dishes is usually one of the least favorite household chores. The good news is that many homes have an appliance called a dishwasher to handle much of the dirty work. So load it up and stop complaining. If you don't have a dishwasher stand at the sink and knock it out. Make sure to put things back in their proper place. If the kitchen adventure is new to you this is no time to reorganize things—your wife's stress levels will definitely go up if you do.

Speaking of dish washing, this may be one corner of your household you can permanently adopt. It has been for me. During one of our pregnancies I noticed this routine chore was something I could do to take the edge off of my wife's workload. So I became the point man on loading and unloading the dishwasher every day. Both my wife and I put things in as they are used throughout the day. Before going to bed in the evening I make sure all the day's remaining dishes are loaded. I put in the soap and set the delay timer to run at night while everyone is sleeping. Before I go to work in the morning I unload it and put everything away. I also load any dirty dishes from the morning breakfast. As your family grows you will have more and more dishes to clean each day so the time involved increases slightly. This is part of getting up earlier each day to get all your chores done. My wife enjoys having this routine task off of her own to-do list.

This particular dishwasher regimen, just like all of your other routines, may need to be adjusted for your schedule and lifestyle. For example, you might need to run the dishwasher during the day instead if it is too loud or it fits your schedule better than a night run. The point is to take this daily task on your shoulders and relieve your wife of it. Remember also that if you sign up for duty you need to stick with it. Don't do it for a week or two and then start to conveniently forget about it. This will do more harm than good, so hang tough and be dependable.

Once you have kitchen clean up mastered, you will want to talk with your wife about other cleaning duties you can handle in the house. Here is a list of some things you might be able to help with:

→ Vacuuming, mopping, and floor cleaning
→ Dusting and wiping down
→ Picking up and putting things away

- Taking out the trash
- Bathroom cleaning: tubs, showers, sinks, toilets, and floors
- Laundry: washing, drying, ironing, and putting away
- Making beds and changing bedding.

Cleaning a house may or may not be your cup of tea. I have heard many men say "no way" to helping clean or "it doesn't bother me" when the house gets out of order. Don't fall into this macho trap. Get over it and figure out where you can get involved.

For those needing some ideas on what to do and how to do it refer to the "How To Clean a House" power module at the back of this book. It will give you some great pointers on how to do a great job and how to get it done *FAST*. If your wife happens to be doing most of the cleaning chores now, another option is to follow her around the house and see how she likes to clean it.

Figure out together where you can carry some of the cooking and cleaning load in your home. Pregnancy is a great time to get into this kind of habit. When the baby arrives you will both have less free time so make sure you stick with your commitment of doing your chores on time. Don't be a flash in the pan and just do it once or twice and then "forget" about it. There is no better way to honor your wife than to clean her bathroom or build killer lasagna on a regular basis.

Other Household Duties

In addition to cooking and cleaning, there are other routine household duties where you can lend a hand if you aren't already. These include:

- Grocery shopping
- Bill paying and money management

- Errand running
- Pet care
- Home maintenance

One of my favorite tasks to share with my wife is grocery shopping. I enjoy making a list of what we need including the ingredients for my latest dinner masterpiece. I also like to buy fun stuff and surprise her with things we might not get every day, such as ice cream cones, a special coffee flavor, or some great bagels for breakfast. So don't be afraid to go to the store and be creative.

> **The key here is commitment. If you say you are going to do something, do it.**

Depending on your household you or your wife may be the exclusive bill payer or you may be sharing the task. If she is carrying some of this load see if you can relieve her. Money matters will be covered in more detail in the next chapter, but see if there is an opportunity for you to help. The key here is commitment. If you say you are going to do something, do it. If you are going to pay the water and electricity bills, do it. Having your utilities turned off because you forgot to pay the bill will not make a pregnant woman happy or decrease her stress levels. If you need some kind of calendar or reminder system to help you, get it and use it.

Another area you might be able to help your wife is running errands. See if you can handle some of the post office, bank, cleaners, or other places she might need to go. Work these into your regular day before or after work or on your lunch break. If you have pets, make sure you are taking on some of the responsibility for their care.

Maintenance around the house is a great place to help out, especially in the area I call "annoyance elimination." Every home, apartment, or car has those little things that for one reason or another go unaddressed. This might include a leaky faucet, a light switch that doesn't work, or a mystery noise in the car. My wife and I experienced a great example. For years we used a coffee pot with a bad design that leaked every time you poured out a cup of coffee. This required us to keep a wet cloth handy to wipe up after every cup of coffee. We both took great joy in finally getting rid of this annoying piece of junk and buying a coffee pot that didn't leak.

You know what the little annoyances are in your own life. Be done with them. Fixing them now during pregnancy is a great way to show some love to your wife and help take some stress out of her day and yours.

Shopping for Baby

Babies require a lot of gear. Before your baby arrives you will acquire everything from the tiniest socks you have ever seen to substantial pieces of furniture. Here are ten of the more costly items you may need to get:

1. Crib
2. Crib mattress, bedding, and bumper pads
3. Diaper changing table
4. Baby monitor
5. Car seat(s) and baby carrier
6. Baby swing
7. Portable playpen
8. Stroller
9. Highchair
10. Video camera

There are several ways to acquire all this equipment. Some of it you may already own. Some may be given or loaned to you by friends or relatives. You may get some as gifts and you will probably have to buy some. Most people get their arsenal through a combination of these sources.

It is likely you and your wife will have to go shopping for some of these items and decide what to buy. If you are lucky enough to have a baby shower, you will hopefully get to pick out and register for the exact items you want. You or your wife may know exactly the brand or look of the items you desire. This is a fun time. But if you don't have clear vision, sometimes it can be hard to sort through it all and decide what to buy.

The key to good purchases is good information. You need to do some research before you head out to the store.

Numerous brands and designs exist in every product category. Take car seats, for example. You can choose from dozens of models. Different designs, brand names, colors, options, and weight ranges can make the first-time buyer's head spin. Interpretation: this can be a stressful time for your wife.

So how can you help? The key, my friend, to good purchases is good information. You need to do some research before you head out to the store. The great news is that there are several places you can get super product advice. Start by asking friends and family with little ones what they like about their various gear choices. Then blend that with one of the various online tools to get another angle.

One of my favorite product information sources is Consumer Reports. In addition to a great monthly magazine, they have an even better website (consumerreports.org) to research everything from soap to strollers, cars to camcorders, and diapers to dryers. It costs only a few dollars for a year's subscription. You can easily make the cost up on your first purchase by being better informed and knowing which products are the best values for the money. They don't accept outside advertising and they thoroughly test every product for you. They also teach you the specific lingo that applies to each product and what you need to know to make the best purchase. Good stuff.

In the end your great information may still lose out to the product that is the cutest, but at least you will know how it compares. So talk with your wife about what purchase or registry items you might want to research. Remember to think into the future as well. Is it possible you will be having more children down the road? If so you might want to get big items like car seats and beds that are more gender neutral in color and design. You don't want to put your brand new strapping baby boy into his older sister's pink car seat, right? You also might want to consider if the car seat and stroller system you buy today is compatible with a double stroller you might have to buy in the future. So dive in, do some research, and think it through. When you head to the stores you and your wife will be less stressed and ready to do battle.

Building and Organizing

Having a baby means Dad gets to put stuff together. Lots of it. Beds, toys, strollers, bookshelves—you name it. So, break out your screwdrivers and your patience; there is lots of work to do.

Some guys like the challenge of tackling boxes of crazy looking parts and building a masterpiece. Others among us are not as excited. Whatever your feelings, take on the job with a joyful heart. Remember these are things for your new baby. So take your time and do a good job.

One tip you will want to keep in mind is your wife's vision for a particular project. Don't let things sit too long while you keep promising to get to it next weekend. That can create stress for everyone. Ask your wife when you are unloading the big project from the car when she would like to have it completed and then agree on a time. She may be fine with a few weeks in some cases, but other times she may want the piece built now. Be patient and work it out.

Here are a few tips to help you keep your sanity in the building and organizing phase:

- →﹒ Establish a file or file box to organize all the owner's manuals, assembly instructions, and receipts. Then when you have a question about the video camera or need to order a replacement part for your stroller years down the road, you will know where to go.
- →﹒ Save time by setting up a small toolbox for home use and keep it separate from your main tool collection. Keep a pair of pliers, an adjustable wrench, a hammer, and a couple of screwdrivers in it. Also a few Ziploc sandwich bags are great for storing any extra parts.
- →﹒ Label and store leftover paint in a safe place. I guarantee your two-year-old will decide to do some decorating of their own on your walls. You will need those leftover paint supplies to cover their creations.

Flip This Room

One big hands-in-the-game project may be the establishment of a baby nursery in your home. Chances are if this is the first baby to arrive at your house you don't have a "cute" and baby friendly room ready to go. There will likely be painting to do, curtains to hang, and more.

My wife and I went through this exercise right before the arrival of our first child. Our first home together was a quaint three-bedroom number in a quiet neighborhood. In addition to our bedroom, we had a spare bedroom for guests and I had a home office in the third bedroom. When we started to plan room use with a larger family, the choice was easy for me. The spare bedroom would go and we would remake it into a nursery. I thought the conversion process would be easy as 1-2-3: (1) remove spare bed, (2) bring in new baby bed, (3) return to couch and watch football.

My wife had a much different vision. You see what I hadn't counted on was *which* room she envisioned the nursery occupying. That room was where my home office was. According to my wife it had the better windows, ceiling height, and layout. She was right; that room was beautiful. I had a big cozy chair, a big beautiful desk with plenty of room to work, and a deer head on the wall. A man's paradise now captured. After some debate and foot dragging on my part, I agreed to relocate my office (and the deer head) to the spare bedroom. Junior would take over the old office room as his nursery. Leadership and love at work.

The moral of the story is to be flexible, patient, and creative as you reconfigure your home for your baby.

When it came time to move the big beautiful desk to the other room, we ran into a challenge. You see I built the desk from a kit, and I built it in the room. Wouldn't you know the desk was too big to fit through the door? And it was glued, screwed, and nailed together quite well, thank you. There was no taking this desk apart again. My office was saved! The baby would have to go in the spare room after all, right?

My favorite video footage of our first pregnancy is me in my office, sawing three inches off the bottom of my big beautiful desk! The moral of the story is to be flexible, patient, and creative as you reconfigure your home for your baby. It all worked out for me and it will for you too. Have fun and enjoy the move.

Baby Correspondence

Having a baby requires a good amount of written correspondence. There can be lots of baby announcements to send, thank you notes to write, envelopes to address, and more. This is another area where Dad can lend a helping hand.

Work with your wife and see where a lumberjack can help. If writing a thank you note for a pretty blanket is not your forte, see if you can handle the envelope chores. Writing out addresses and sticking stamps can be one of those little things that helps take the edge off of your wife's workload. Make it a fun team project as you sit around the kitchen table and work on it together. It's a great time to talk about all of the other baby topics.

Here are some additional ideas for helping with correspondence:

→ If you are handy with the computer and spreadsheets, make an address database of all family and friends. That way you can quickly generate mailing labels for thank you notes, invitations, announcements, and Christmas cards.
→ Buy a spiral notebook and start a thank you note log of who got you what gift. This will help you make sure nothing slips through the cracks. Make sure you take this to the hospital so you can record gifts and flowers that arrive there.
→ Volunteer to be the stamp buyer and the guy who gets the correspondence to the mailbox.

One last word of advice on correspondence: if you volunteer to help, make sure you get your job done on time. Ahead of time would be even better. You don't want your wife's stack of completed notes waiting on you to fill out the envelopes. Get in there and get it done. Remember, leadership and love.

Let's Get 'er Done

So, when are you going to do all of this cooking, cleaning, shopping, errand running, building, organizing, and envelope licking?

On your lunch break. Before you go to bed. Early in the morning (my personal favorite). Whenever you can. The important thing is to adjust your schedule, get in there, start doing some new things, and stick to your commitments.

One of my favorite movie classics is *Top Gun* starring Tom Cruise. In part of the movie, hotshot Navy pilot Maverick, played by Cruise, is emotionally lost after losing his partner Goose in a plane crash. Maverick can't seem to let his old life go; he keeps holding on to Goose—even physically holding onto his dog tags. When new tests and battles come up Maverick won't get in the game. In pilot terms, he won't *engage*. He is stalled with all kinds of excuses: the timing isn't right, the set up isn't perfect, and the people around him aren't perfect. Not until he lets a piece of his old life go (Goose) does he finally grab the new situations and challenges and get after them.

Just like Maverick, you must engage in the battle at hand: getting things done. Don't be paralyzed by how and when you have done things in the past. Don't wait for the perfect time or situation. Your wife needs a fully engaged partner with head and hands in the game. And she needs it now. Get in there "Mav" and get it done.

FATHER, bless my body and my hands to take on extra work and responsibility during this time. Bless me with new skills and the ability to get things done. Let each hour of sleep I get be doubled in its rejuvenating strength. Let my wife be more relaxed as we prepare our home and our lives for this child. Bless the health and spirit of each member of this growing family. In the name of the One who engages with us in all things big and small, **AMEN.**

Wisdom to Consider

"There are risks and costs to a program of action. But they are far less than the long-range risks and costs of comfortable inaction."

JOHN F. KENNEDY

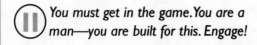 *You must get in the game. You are a man—you are built for this. Engage!*

☑ CHAPTER CHECKLIST

❏ Have a healthy conversation with your wife about things you can do around the house to help. Explain that you want to help and want to take on some new tasks to help lighten the load for her.

❏ Find some recipes you can handle in the kitchen. Run them by your wife and see if they sound good to her. Perfect a few and make them regularly.

❏ Become "Captain of the Dishwasher." Load it at night and unload it in the morning. If you don't have a dishwasher, make sure you have washed and put away everything before heading out to work each day.

❏ Talk with your wife and assume at least one regular household cleaning task if not more. If the bathroom is yours to handle, strive to do it with excellence. Do it fast, do it regularly, and do it with a smile.

❏ Pick out some other household chores you can do on a regular basis, such as errand running or grocery shopping. Keep your commitments and have fun with them.

❏ Eliminate the small annoyances in your home like leaky faucets, squeaky doors, clutter, and things that don't work.

❏ Research some of your bigger baby purchases, such as car seats, video cameras, and strollers. Have the information with you when you head to the store or shop online.

❏ Subscribe to Consumer Reports online version at www.consumerreports.org.

❑ Get new purchases or gifts put together quickly. Set up a file box for manuals and organize your toolbox.

❑ Help your wife "build" the nursery area of your home. Be flexible and open-minded. Remember to properly store and label those leftover paint supplies.

❑ Help your wife with the baby correspondence of thank you notes, announcements, and envelopes. Get your assignments and finish them ahead of the agreed upon deadline.

❑ Try new things. Partner with your wife and find out where you can get your hands in the game on a regular basis. Insist that you help. Take the edges off of her task load. Engage!

Chapter 4

Getting Your Wallet in the Game

▶ Diapers. Doctors. Formula. Food. Clothes. College. The list goes on and on. Your baby will require all these things and more. And they all have one thing in common: they cost money. Bringing a child into the world is an expensive proposition. Based on data from the U.S. Department of Agriculture's report, "Expenditures on Children by Families, 2006," from birth to age eighteen the average child will cost more than $260,000.00 to raise.[3] If you want to add leather seats, power windows, and a four-year college degree, you are looking at an additional $200,000.00. [4] Wow! And you think cars and big-screen TVs are expensive.

The good news is you don't have to write that check the day your child is born. You have eighteen years to "finance" it and pay-as-you-go terms. The other good news is that millions of people have walked the same path before you and done it successfully. You can too. And the best news of all is that your return on investment is huge: a lasting legacy. Along the way you get to enjoy hugs, homeruns, graduations, grandkids, and much more.

The keys to handling baby finances are the same as tackling any other big project in life. You need to manage it and have good information. In this chapter we cover the basics, but the uniqueness of your own situation may require you to dig deeper in some areas. An unlimited number of books and other resources are out there on money management. Go find the additional information and people who will help you get a handle on your finances.

Hands down money issues are the number one cause of marital problems today in America. As you prepare to bring a baby into the world, you and your wife need to be communicating on money matters like never before. These little people cost a boatload and if you aren't on the same page it will be hard on your marriage. So talk with your spouse, share your feelings and ideas, and get it all on the table. It's okay if you don't have the prettiest balance sheet on the block. You both need to know where you are and what your priorities, goals, and plans for action are. If you are at odds over money, your and your wife's stress levels will be high, which is not a good thing. Be together on all things relating to money and your stress levels will be lower.

> *Be together on all things relating to money and your stress levels will be lower.*

While money and financial matters can be complicated it helps to break things down and make it simple. To do this keep your eyes on the three "I's": income, insurance, and investment. Gaining more knowledge about each of these will help you set some goals and put some good action plans in place.

The first is income. It is where you will spend most of your day-to-day time and also includes managing expenses and a budget. The second I is insurance. This family of products helps protect from the unpredictable events in life that can crash your financial plans. The third I is investment—preparing for your future needs and your baby's future needs.

1. Income

The birth of a baby is a great time to do a life check-up and ask some questions. Does our household have an adequate income? Will we be a 1, 1.5, or 2-income household? If we both work, who will take care of the children and how much will it cost? Where do we want to be financially in a year? In five years? In twenty years? These are questions that deserve some thought and discussion with your wife.

Staying at Home

One of the most sought after jobs in America today is the stay-at-home parent. If you can swing it financially, it benefits the child (and the parents) in many different ways. The stay-at-home parent has traditionally been the mother, but more and more fathers are taking on the role.

Don't confuse "stay at home" with "easy." The stay-at-home parent will be on his or her feet most of the day taking care of the child and keeping a handle on the increased load of household chores. This is not a bon-bon-eating-couch-riding assignment. It is hard work both mentally and physically.

If your finances or other circumstances dictate both parents working, it certainly isn't the end of the world. Kids in this situation are going to be fine and the parents will be too. But make sure you are truly winning financially with both parents working outside the home. Sit down and take a hard look at the net dollars in your pocket the second working spouse contributes. Look at the take home pay each month after taxes. Then take the expenses out of that amount required to earn it. A big one might be child daycare. Next you should subtract transportation costs, clothing or uniform expenses, and other costs depending on the line of work.

After you do the math look at the net contribution of the second working parent. If it is the significant amount you need, you now have your answer. But if the amount is not that big, you might reconsider and get a little creative in the process. Plenty of couples are able to reconfigure their lifestyle so one parent can stay home. In some cases it means fewer vacations and less eating out to make it work. Or a less expensive car so there's no car payment. Or the stay-at-home spouse does some part-time work in the evening or on weekends. I know several couples where the working parent takes a second job in the evening delivering pizza so the other parent can be at home with their small children.

> *Not having a budget is like driving down a dark road without your headlights.... Sooner or later you will crash.*

If you decide that having one parent at home is a priority then put your heads together and see if you can make it work. With some sacrifice and creativity it just might be the best decision you ever made.

Get a Plan, Stan

Well-known financial expert and author Dave Ramsey tells us repeatedly to spend our money on paper before we spend it for real. In other words, put together a written budget and stick to it. Not having a budget is like driving down a dark road without your headlights. You can't see where you are going, and sooner or later you will crash.

Money just seems to disappear fast with babies in the house. For example, if you are using disposable diapers you should plan for an additional $50.00 to $100.00 per month for those. If you already have kids in diapers, you know the impact adding another will have on this part of your budget. If you don't have a fix on the dollars coming in and going out you can quickly get into trouble.

Budget often gets linked with other bummer words, such as *party pooper, crime record, rigid,* or *impossible.* If this is the case for you or your spouse, then move from bummer to better and call it a plan, priority list, or financial road map. These are more descriptive anyway and paint a better picture of what you are trying to do.

So how do you do a budget / plan / priority list / financial road map? Look first at your monthly average take-home money. Next look at your monthly expenses and outflow. Here are some categories to consider (your own situation will dictate others):

- → Housing—mortgage or rent
- → Utilities—water, electricity, natural gas, trash pick-up
- → Phone—land line and/or cellular
- → TV and computer service
- → Groceries and household supplies
- → Insurance costs—health, home, auto, life, disability
- → Tithing and giving
- → Clothing
- → Transportation—gas, parking, car costs
- → Entertainment—eating out, movies, and so on
- → Child care
- → Baby costs—diapers, clothing, and formula
- → Health care— doctor visits, prescriptions, other
- → HOK (Heaven Only Knows)—haircuts, presents, other, and so forth
- → Savings—retirement, college, other
- → "Blow" money (others may call it "mad" money)
- → Debt repayment—car loans, student loans, credit cards

Look back at several months of bills and receipts and see if you can come up with the average you have spent in each category. Some months will be different for each category, but for now just try to get an average. As you do this you will be able to see where your money has *gone in the past*. This is the first step in gaining control of where it will *go in the future*.

Add up your monthly expenses/outflow and see how it compares to your net income. If you have income left over, then you have the fun part of deciding how best to utilize that for the future. If your initial draft of expenses and spending has more points on the board than income, then you have some work to do.

The next step in working your plan is to know which plan categories you have the most control over. For example, you don't have as much short-term control of your rent or mortgage payment as you do the amount you spend on clothing, eating out, or blowing. You could adjust your rent or mortgage by moving, but it isn't something you will choose to do every day.

Next, analyze the big drains in those day-to-day categories. For example, our family of five struggles to control the day-to-day categories of groceries, clothing, and entertainment/eating out. It takes real discipline and some sacrifice to keep these in line for us.

Keep massaging and prioritizing categories in your plan until it fits inside the income.

At some point you may realize you have an income problem and need to find a way to push that up. Again, the important part is to drive the dollar road with your lights on and know what corrections to make.

So how do you make your plan work consistently? The key is to stick with the amounts you budget in each category. And don't spend next month's budget for something you want this month. That never works. You and your wife must be in agreement on all of these amounts for the plan to work. Talk through it until you both are comfortable.

A key for many people is having a little "blow money." Depending on your budget, this is money you can spend without accounting for. It is meant to be a relief valve in spending for all of the other categories in which you are exercising so much discipline. This is the category for your $4.00 cup of coffee.

Debt Control

One of the main reasons you need a plan is to avoid the big marital strain of debt. The pain and worry of excess debt can be overwhelming. The Bible states in Proverbs 22:7, "the borrower is servant to the lender." Yikes. None of us want to be in that position.

A ton of information is available on debt and how to eliminate it but there is one age-old truth that is the foundation of it all. That is to live within your means—or spend less than you earn. Sounds easy enough, but it takes hard work, discipline, sacrifice, and lots of open communication in your marriage. These are the same things bringing a new baby into the family requires, so you may as well tackle both at the same time.

Financial guru Ramsey also offers up a straight ahead plan for getting out of debt and building a bright financial future. The first thing you need to do, after building your budget, is pay for essential living expenses like food, shelter, utilities, and basic transportation. After that Ramsey's "Seven Baby Steps" go like this and must be accomplished in order:[5]

1. Set up an emergency fund of $1,000.00 cash for life's unexpected events.
2. Pay off debts from smallest to largest. Be sure to go after the smallest first to get that feeling of accomplishment when it is paid.
3. Build your emergency fund up to three to six months of living expenses.
4. Invest 15 percent of household income into Roth IRAs and pre-tax retirement accounts like a 401K.
5. Save for the college education of your children.
6. Pay off your home mortgage early.
7. Build wealth and give.

While your own circumstances are unique, this basic progression should be the foundation for walking through life. It is important to finish each step before moving on to the next. It doesn't make sense for example to save for college while you are paying an interest-only payment on a big credit card debt.

There are a few other things to keep in mind as you go. First, be wary of car debt. Many people are in love with cars. But car payments (yes, any car payment) can literally suck the life out of the best-laid financial plans.

Use common sense and don't let the emotions of your growing family take over.

I know one couple paying nearly $1,000.00 each month in car payments and they still can't figure out why they are struggling financially. If you need to downgrade what you drive for a while, do it. Save up and pay cash to upgrade. With a baby in the house you will understandably want to have a safe and reliable car, but that doesn't mean it has to be brand new.

Next you want to be wary of the same love trap with a house. Many couples, especially those with new babies, want a house or place to live with more room. This is a worthy desire, but not if it hammers your budget to the point it causes stress in your marriage. A good rule of thumb is your mortgage or rent payment should not exceed 25 percent of your monthly take home pay. Plenty of couples have a big, beautiful house but are so financially strained by it they are miserable. Use common sense and don't let the emotions of your growing family take over. Comfort and safety will be high on your wife's priority list, so make sure you balance it all with your decisions as a couple.

The final thing to keep in mind is actually the first thing you should do in working with finances, and that is tithing and giving. It is emotionally and spiritually important for couples to give back a portion of what they earn—not so much because the church or charity needs that particular contribution, but because something within each of us needs to give. Tithing and giving needs to be part of your plan.

Success in baby finances will come by managing both income and expenses. Make sure you and your wife talk about both and that you are together on your plans. Then go out and get it done.

2. Insurance

With a baby on board it is more important then ever to do a thorough checkup of each type of insurance coverage. Before we analyze each type of coverage, let's look at why we need this expensive, complex product called insurance in the first place.

The goal most people have for finances is to steadily improve their situation through the working years, to successfully raise their children, to retire with dignity, and to be self-supporting. The tough part is the road of life is full of bumps and collisions that can set a family back financially—way back. Some setbacks can hurt for a month, some for a year, and some for a lifetime. Everyone needs insurance—whether for home, health, life, or stuff—to avoid financial hardship and the stress it brings to bear.

It is your job as the leader of your family to ensure your insurance portfolio is stocked with what you need. Before Baby you may have opted to skimp or not even have certain coverage at all. That won't work now. This little person is depending entirely on you for protection, food, and life's other necessities. If something happens to you they can't go out and get a job to support themselves. They are counting on you and they don't understand excuses.

Health Insurance

With a baby on the way or already in the house, this is your most immediate need. Health insurance will help pay for the expense of delivery, which can range from $5,000 to $10,000 for a normal, uncomplicated one. On the other end, if you have a premature baby who comes along a couple of months early, you can easily top $100,000 in expenses. Without insurance, that amount could be a lifelong financial issue for you and your family.

Another advantage that health insurance brings in most cases is the power of negotiated discounts with doctors and hospitals. If you go into a hospital without insurance you may have to pay the full price. Go in with health insurance and you will be starting from the discounted price.

Health insurance will also help you weather the storm if any problems arise long after delivery. My wife and I experienced this with the birth of our third child. Our daughter was born full term and had a very normal delivery. One month after birth she developed complications and required hospitalization, testing, and follow-up care. By the time she was two years old, she had more than seventy separate medical encounters, amounting to tens of thousands of dollars in expenses. When your baby is sick you want to see the best doctors on the planet—and they cost lots of money. Without medical insurance our family would have been financially devastated. Our health insurance saved us. While the vast majority of babies are born and grow up with no complications, it is your job as the family leader to guard against the most devastating financial circumstances. That means having some kind of health insurance coverage.

Choices

If you or your wife are covering the family through one of your employer's plans, your choices are easier. You may have one or several plan options to choose from. It is yours and your wife's job to analyze the available plans and make the most informed choice possible.

In looking at your employer's plans, make sure you are looking at all costs involved. This will include the amount coming out of your paycheck. It also includes your cost sharing as dictated by the plan, such as deductibles, copayments, and coinsurance. If you need help understanding your cost obligation with a baby coming talk to your employer or call the insurance company and have them walk you through it. Make sure your coverage is in force and that any required paperwork for the upcoming hospital stay is in on time to the insurance company.

It is your job as the family leader to guard against the most devastating financial circumstances.

The other thing to consider is the choice of providers available in the plans. You will need to consider what physicians you and your wife want to use and which hospital handles the delivery. In nearly all cases you will want to be using providers in the insurance network. Again, if you need help figuring this out go to your employer or the insurance company.

If you or your wife don't have insurance available through your employer, you still have some options. You may be able to purchase an individual health insurance policy. These days all sorts are available, including traditional plans and Health Savings Accounts. The best way to figure these products out is to hire someone to do it for you. Seek out the services of an independent insurance agent who can look at your situation and your budget and give you options from several reputable companies. Depending on your qualifications, your state government may also be a source for coverage.

Other types of coverage you will run into in the health category include dental, vision, cancer, and critical illness coverage. If your employer offers dental and vision, they are usually worth considering. Both of these plans can help smooth out your expenses in these areas from year to year. Unlike health problems, dental and eyeglass problems are not likely to be catastrophic. If you have needs in these areas the coverage can be a great value and help your budgeting. Cancer and critical illness policies are another story. If you have good health and disability insurance and an emergency fund, these products aren't worth the cost.

No health insurance plan comes cheap these days. Remember you are protecting your family's future. Don't gamble here. You need some level of coverage, even if it just protects you from the large catastrophic expenses.

Life Insurance

Most adults should have some life insurance. Anyone who has a dependent child or is expecting a child MUST have life insurance—and a lot of it. You would be surprised at the number of couples marching through life with little or no life insurance. Typical reasons for this are not fully thinking through the consequences, not knowing how to shop for it, and not knowing how much to purchase.

Let's first understand the purpose of life insurance and the consequences it protects against. In the unlikely event you die, a life insurance policy will provide a sum of money to the people you designate—your beneficiaries. This money helps replace your biggest financial asset: the ability to earn an income. This money will help provide food, clothing, housing, college educations, and more. This is money your family needs to survive.

Think through the consequences if you died today. It can be uncomfortable thinking, but you only need to do it once so get it done. Picture your surviving spouse. While suffering tremendous grief she has to sit down by herself at the kitchen table and answer questions like these for the family: how will we eat, how will I pay the rent or mortgage, where will I work, how will I make ends meet, who will take care of the children while I work, and how will I take care of the family financially for all the years ahead?

These are brutal questions. Questions no grieving spouse should have to answer. Adequate life insurance takes these questions off of the table. Life insurance allows your spouse to focus her energy on more important topics, such as healing her own grief and caring for the children. In your marriage ceremony you commit to care for your spouse as long as you BOTH shall live—not as long as only YOU shall live. Your commitment to care for your spouse and family doesn't end when you die. You are supposed to take care of these people whether you are on the planet or not. Unless you already have a million or two in the bank, life insurance is the one tool that provides the financial power to get this done. More than anything life insurance gives the surviving spouse options, like continuing the role as a stay at home parent while the children are young. No life insurance can mean no options. And that means the surviving spouse has to immediately go to work or stay working and slug it out on her own.

Your commitment to care for your spouse and family doesn't end when you die.

My own father died in a tragic work related accident when I was a child. He understood the promise to provide and had ample life insurance in place. It allowed our family to pick up the pieces of our shattered lives and put them back together. It allowed for a smooth transition of a family business. It allowed me to go to college, which in turn opened more doors for me. Life insurance changed my life. You need to make sure you are giving your family the security and opportunity they deserve.

Amounts and Flavors

So how much and what kind of life insurance do you need? Let's tackle these questions one at a time. First, let's figure out what kind of life insurance you should get. Hundreds of life insurance companies manufacture dozens of product styles. The good news is you can quickly boil this down. Here are three things to look for:

1. Buy twenty-year term life. Do not waste your money on various whole life products that promise an income stream later in life or cash value. Term life will cover you while your children are being raised and counting on your income. Once the children are out of the house you can reassess your position and see what amount of insurance you still need.

2. Buy from a life insurance company with an "A.M. Best" rating of *A* or better. Best assigns financial ratings to these companies and is a good indication of the strength and staying power of a firm.

3. Buy from a life insurance company with at least $100 billion of coverage already in-force. This will put you with a sizeable company focused on the business.

To get the best buying experience possible you should seek out a qualified life insurance sales person. Ask for referrals from friends, coworkers, or your church. Find an agent who can get you quotes from several companies and most importantly someone with whom you feel comfortable dealing. Most of the people selling these products are good people, but there are a few bad apples in every barrel. Choose your coverage from someone who has been in the insurance profession for at least five years and is making a full-time living at it. Remember this will be the person your wife will be looking to for assistance should something happen to you. It needs to be a professional you can count on.

If you are already savvy with the products and have had life insurance before, you may want to consider shopping for coverage via the Internet. The same rules for choosing a company apply. With many companies the rates are the same whether you do it yourself online or with a qualified agent. I usually recommend using an agent. An agent can help you navigate the application and approval process and answer any questions you have, thus removing some of the anxiety in the process.

How Much

So, how much life insurance should you buy? Remember that twenty-year level term insurance is the product to seek. The amount you need is fairly straightforward when you break it down like this: the amount should be large enough to generate annual proceeds that equal or exceed your current income.

In other words you need an *engine* that creates enough income each year for your family to live, without reducing the size of the engine. A good life insurance representative can help you through a calculation of how much. One rule of thumb that has been around for a while is to purchase an amount equal to eight to ten times your annual income.

I like fifteen times your annual income even better, and here's why. Let's say you are making $50,000.00 per year. Fifteen times that amount would be $750,000.00 in coverage. If your wife invested that money wisely with a professional advisor and made a 7 percent annual return, she would have $52,500.00 in income each year.

For more than eighty years the stock market has produced an average annual return of more than 10 percent when adjusted for inflation. With professional management I believe that 10 percent is a good target to shoot for. The extra 3 percent earnings above the 7 percent she needs to live on would be reinvested to help counter inflation. Now the engine is growing slightly each year and so are the net proceeds, which will solve the inflation problem.

A good financial planner or life insurance agent can really help you solve your specific situation. The bottom line is to get a good solid amount of coverage in place and not to agonize over how much. To really boil it down, I believe every father in the United States should have at least $500,000.00 in coverage and most should have a $1 million.

So how much does all this life insurance cost? A big life insurance policy must be expensive, right? The great news is that it isn't. A typical thirty-year-old male in good health should be able to find a $1million policy for less than $50.00 per month, and a $500,000.00 policy for less than $25.00 per month. Expect to pay more if you are older, a smoker, or have some health conditions. The key is to shop around and get quotes from several companies. There is a lot of competition in the insurance business and you can reap the benefit.

Spouse Coverage

Many couples do a great job insuring the primary bread-winner, but they may forget to adequately insure the spouse or the stay-at-home parent. Take my situation. My wife is a stay-at-home mom for our three children, and she runs a small in-home business on the side. If she died our family would still require all of the hours she provides caring for the family and her income. I would have to spend much more time at home holding the family together. I may have to hire some part-time help to get us through as well. I would have to cut back my hours at work and possibly even change jobs to make sure I had adequate at-home time. A life insurance policy would help make up for the decrease in income and the added expense of hiring some help. We would require even more coverage if I wanted the option of staying at home full time.

Think through what options you would want to have and then get the proper amount of coverage for your spouse. As a rule of thumb, your wife should have no less than half the coverage you have.

Disability Insurance

Another tool that helps protect your biggest financial asset (the ability to earn an income for your family) is disability insurance. It provides a stream of income

Thirty percent of all Americans between the ages of thirty-five and sixty-five will become disabled at least once for more than ninety days during their working lives.

while you are unable to perform your normal job duties because of an illness or injury. According to the Council of Life Insurers, 30 percent of all Americans between the ages of thirty-five and sixty-five will become disabled at least once for more than ninety days during their working lives. Your chances of becoming disabled are much higher than your chances of dying. Nobody wants to face the prospects of losing their home because they are sick or injured, yet more than 40 percent of all foreclosures on conventional mortgages are brought about by a disability. Disability insurance helps protect you and your family in these situations.

Disability insurance comes in two flavors: short term and long term. Short-term disability typically covers you after you have been out of work for sickness or injury for a period of time, usually seven to fourteen days. It will kick in and pay a percentage of your normal income. Policies and limitations will vary.

Long-term disability covers you for—you guessed it—longer periods of time off because of illness or injury. These policies usually kick in after 90 to 120 days and pay a percentage of your normal income. These policies and limitations will also vary.

If your employer offers these plans make sure you are signed up and they are in force. If your employer doesn't offer disability coverage or if you are self-employed, you will need to seek out an individual long-term disability policy. Your life insurance agent may be able to help you in this area as well. Be sure to shop several companies for the best value as these policies can get pricey.

The possibility of being unable to work for a period of time due to a disability is another great reason to have an emergency fund of three to six months' living expenses stashed away. The emergency fund will come into play not only if your refrigerator quits working but also if you drop the new refrigerator on your foot and can't work.

Property Insurance

Having a baby is the perfect time to do an evaluation of your property insurance. This is the category of coverage for your bigger assets, most typically your home and your cars.

Homeowner's coverage is vital. It will protect you from financial disaster should you suffer a loss from fire, theft, or Mother Nature. If you are a renter you absolutely need similar coverage called renter's insurance. Even though as a renter you don't own the property or structure, you still need to protect your contents. Don't risk taking a pass on this coverage just because you don't think you own much of real value. The replacement cost of all your family's clothes, furniture, and household possessions can be huge. And with a baby you have even more gear to cover.

Make sure you have other coverage for your own unique situation if necessary. This might include special coverage for your business, tools, jewelry, or any collections you own and want to protect.

Here are ten tips to help you protect your family, home, and assets:

1. Have working smoke detectors throughout your home or apartment. You need one in every main area and one in every bedroom.

2. Install at least one carbon monoxide detector as well.

3. Consider a monitored home security system to deter burglars. Statistics show thieves are two to three times less likely to target your home if it is monitored. Good systems are typically available for less than twenty dollars per month.

4. If you decide not to get a home security system, at least get some alarm monitoring stickers from you local hardware store and put them on your doors and windows. This can deter some thieves who don't want to take a chance.

5. Replace the hoses on your washing machine at least every five years. Burst washing machine hoses are a leading cause of home floods.

6. Have the dryer vent cleaned on your clothes dryer every couple of years to reduce the risk of fire.

7. Know where the main shutoffs are for water, gas, and electricity coming into your home.

8. Purchase at least three good fire extinguishers for your home. Install them throughout the home where they are easy to get. Make sure your wife knows where they are and that you both know how to use them.

9. Buy a fireproof safety box to store important papers. Put your marriage license, life insurance, birth certificates, and other important items in there.

10. Videotape the contents of your home annually. Be sure to video everywhere including inside closets, drawers, and cabinets. Store the tape with a relative, at work, or in another safe place away from your home. If you ever have a loss you will have a good reminder of the contents of your home for insurance purposes.

If you haven't gotten competitive quotes on your home, auto, and other property coverage in awhile, you should. Call around and get some numbers with the same levels of coverage and deductibles. Then compare them with what you are paying now. Talk with the company or agent where you have your current coverage and tell them you are considering changing carriers. See if they can help you save some money. Look at different deductibles or combining policies with one company to get discounts. If you aren't satisfied, move your coverage.

Wills and Other Legal Documents

No discussion of insurance and protecting your family's future is complete without stressing the important need for a will. A will is a legal document that allows you to spell out the rights of others over your property and children after your death. You and your wife each need one. Shop around and find a good attorney who can prepare these documents for you at a reasonable price.

One of the key items to designate in your will is the legal guardian of your children should you and your wife die at the same time. Of course if only one of you should die, the surviving spouse would care for the children. But in case you both pass away at the same time, you don't want to leave it up to the courts to decide who will care for your children. They may pick somebody you wouldn't. Have a serious discussion with your wife and agree on who the designated guardian will be. Check with that person and make sure he or she is willing to serve as guardian in the unlikely event they are called upon. Review your will each year and keep it current, including the guardian selection. Circumstances and people can change, and this important document must keep up.

You should also work with that same attorney to prepare your living will and health care power of attorney. These two documents are called advance health care directives. A living will allows you to express your wishes concerning life-sustaining procedures. A health care power of attorney allows you to designate a person to make health care decisions on your behalf if you are unable to do so. Again, you and your wife each need to have these documents.

Your specific situation and preferences may require other estate planning tools such as trusts and additional types of power of attorney. Consult with a qualified legal expert on what you need. At a minimum every parent needs a will and the advance health care directives. Spend the time and money to get them done.

3. Investment

The third *I* of our three-legged finance stool is investment, or saving for future needs. Your individual circumstance will dictate the specifics of your short and long-term savings plans.

Babies need lots of money and are a great reason to save. One simple but effective way to save for this impending joy is to get an envelope, write Baby Fund on it, and start putting extra money into it. My wife and I did this as soon as we started talking about kids. By sticking twenty dollars a week in it, or whatever we could spare, we had a nice nest egg by delivery time. We used it to buy a baby bed, changing table, and some other needed items. Take the leadership initiative to set this up and get your wife on board. It is fun to check the progress and think about the best ways to spend it.

The two long-term investment plans you need to be working on are your retirement and your children's college education. Volumes of information are available on each. You may be well on your way in both categories or just thinking about them for the first time. Whatever the case let's take a high level look and provide some basics on each.

Retirement: Making Sure Your Golden Years Aren't Spent in the Red

Bulletin: One of the best gifts you can give your children is confidence they will not have to financially support you in your later years. This is huge, and it is your responsibility to take care of it. And the way you take care of it is to make sure you are investing NOW for your retirement later.

Don't count on Social Security. By the time you get there it may be a much-revised program. Even if it is there it is unlikely it will support you and your wife entirely and allow you to live with the dignity you deserve. What you should count on instead is your own personal retirement savings program.

One of the most popular retirement savings vehicles today is employer sponsored 401K or 403B plans. Having a baby is a great time to do a checkup on your retirement plan at work. In many cases your employer matches your contributions up to certain amounts. You need to make sure you are contributing enough to at least get all of the matching dollars. It is essentially free money.

Make sure the investments you are in are good ones. Unless you are within five years of retirement, you should be in good aggressive growth or growth and income mutual funds. Check the three, five, and ten-year performance of your fund choices and pick ones that have a good track record. Keep a regular watch on these and move your money to other funds if yours starts to suck wind.

Another good retirement savings tool is the ROTH IRA. Most individuals can set up a ROTH and contribute after tax earnings. Check with a good financial planner if you need to set one up. Again, pick out some good mutual funds and start putting money in. The most convenient way is to have an automatic monthly transfer from your checking or other account into the IRA. The key to a good, pain free investment program is to make it automatic so you don't have to think about it.

There are other good retirement savings vehicles out there including SEPs, Traditional IRAs, and more. If you need help figuring it all out, and most people do, get a good financial planner to help you. Unless you are a master at it, keep it simple and easy. Stay away from deals that are too good to be true and stay away from lousy investments like whole life insurance and annuities.

Raising kids is expensive. Times will come when you run out of money before you run out of month. But starting an investment plan for your retirement and sticking with it will reward you and your wife handsomely. You will be able to enjoy yourselves and celebrate all of the hard work you invested in your children. You will have the money to visit your children and your grandchildren wherever they may live. But most importantly you will have given your children the gift of confidence knowing you are financially strong in your retirement. And, you will give them a great example to repeat for their children. Take the lead.

College: Hi Ho, Hi Ho, It's Off to School They Go

It seems a college degree is more necessary than ever to compete for the best jobs. It's going to be even more competitive when your children enter the workforce. And like many other areas of raising kids, you want to have options available for them. So it should be with college. You should strive to give your children the option of going to college with your financial support. Lack of money shouldn't be any child's excuse for not attending college.

Now, does that mean you have to sock away enough dough to get Junior a four-year ride at Harvard? Probably not. That is a tall order to fill. Consider that if you started college today, a four-year degree at a public university, including room and board, will cost an average of $70,000.00. Make that $140,000.00 for a degree from your average private university. Those figures sound like mountains of money.

The real shocker is the inflation for a college education, which currently increases at about twice the regular inflation rate. Increases have averaged 5 percent to 8 percent each year across the country. So if you apply that to our earlier numbers and cast them eighteen years into the future, you are looking at $200,000.00 for four years at a public university and $400,000.00 at a private institution. If your bundle of joy desires to be a doctor or lawyer or wants to get a masters degree, you will get to hear the cash register ring for several more years.

So what are you supposed to do? First and foremost, don't freak out! Nobody said you had to pay for the whole thing. Most kids today get through with a combination of parent support, scholarships, grants, loans, and working their tails off at part-time jobs. The key is to show support and to show there is a way to do it. Show leadership. Kids who see you have some skin in the game with your own dollars will be more motivated.

College Savings Strategy

The big savings weapon you have on your side is time. You should have at least eighteen years to get some money tucked away before the tuition bills start rolling in. Your friend along the way is compound interest that will help your money grow. Consider this: if you invest just $25.00 a month for eighteen years and earn an average return of 10 percent, you will have built up $15,000.00. If you can sock away $100.00 per month, that would balloon to $60,000.00 in eighteen years. The key is to set up an automatic investment that occurs each month. If you don't touch or see the money, you won't even notice it is gone.

Make sure the other financial pieces discussed earlier are in order before aggressively funding a college savings program. Have your emergency funds in place and all debts beside your mortgage taken care of. It doesn't make sense to save for college while you have a credit card balance with 25 percent interest charges. Get your plan and work it.

Several good investment vehicles exist for higher education. The U.S. government likes a nation full of well educated people—so the tax code is set up to motivate you to save. The top two education savings tools are the Education IRA and the 529 College Savings plan. Each has its pros and cons. A good financial planner can help you through the choices and get you set up.

The state run 529 plans have particularly good flexibility in that funds can be moved between children or even saved

Saving for your child's college: First and foremost, don't freak out! Nobody said you had to pay for the whole thing.

for grandchildren if you end up with excess. They can also be used for private schooling if necessary before college. Your choice of investments is dictated by the plan but usually provide enough diversity. Education IRAs are locked into the child's name, so the flexibility isn't as good. But you do get an unlimited choice of investments.

As with most investment plans, it works best to start simple and go from there. As your knowledge grows you can get more sophisticated if you want. Here are some other ideas to consider as you think about college savings:

1. If you are struggling with a monthly commitment, consider socking away any income tax return money you get for education.
2. Remind any friends or family members that college fund donations are always appreciated at birthdays and Christmas. Don't get too crazy with this (kids need toys too), but college dollars have a lifetime impact.
3. If you have a mortgage, do everything you can to get it to a fifteen-year payment schedule. That way when your kids

hit college your home will be paid off and you will have some breathing room in your budget to help.

4. Don't tell your kids at any age they will have to get athletic or academic scholarships if they want to go to college. Kids don't need the pressure and will excel more without it. They should certainly go after scholarships, and if they do land some it will be icing on the cake.

So there you have the three *I*'s of baby finance: income, insurance, and investment. There are lots of choices out there and things to do, so you need to get with it. Remember to make a budget with your wife and stick to it, seek professional advice when necessary, and prepare for life's curve balls. If you give it your best shot you and your family will be greatly rewarded.

FATHER, bless the finances of this growing family. Provide us with a steady abundance and with the tools to manage it wisely. Give us the courage and strength to get out of debt and to save. Bless our minds with good decision-making and our bodies with the energy and will to work extra hard. Give us peace, confidence, and togetherness in all money matters. In the name of the One who provides all we pray, **AMEN.**

Wisdom to Consider

"A father carries pictures where his money used to be."

ANONYMOUS

Children are the best investment you will ever make. Work hard, be smart, and think ahead.

☑ CHAPTER CHECKLIST

❑ Vow to work together with your wife on all money matters. Do not let money bring undue strife to your marriage.

❑ Consider carefully if one parent can park his or her career and stay at home with the children. Look at the income and expenses associated with both parents working. Be creative with part-time work and household expenses.

❑ Spend every dollar on paper before you spend it for real. Build a workable budget, including expenses for Baby and stick with it. Know what money you have coming in and going out. Watch for trouble spots and being in love with high cost cars and houses.

❑ Work on getting out of debt. Put together a plan that will get you out and keep you out. Win here and your marriage will be relieved of a huge stressor.

❑ Get your health insurance lined up for delivery. Know what coverage you have and what your responsibilities are in paperwork and cost sharing. Make sure you have at least some coverage in case your wife or baby has complications.

❑ Buy adequate twenty-year level term life insurance from a reputable insurance agent. Buy ten to fifteen times the current annual income for the main breadwinner and buy at least half that much for the other spouse. Do it now.

❑ Protect your ability to earn a consistent income with disability insurance. Buy it through work if possible or on your own. At the same time make sure you are building a strong emergency fund of three to six months of living expenses. If you are paying off some debt, get an emergency fund of $1,000.00 locked away, pay off the debt, and then build your larger emergency fund.

❑ Evaluate your property insurance for home, auto, and other assets. If you rent make sure you have renter's insurance. Shop around and make sure you have good rates and good coverage.

❑ Ensure your home is a safe place to live. Install good working fire extinguishers, smoke detectors, and carbon monoxide detectors. Look for potential trouble spots in plumbing and electrical. Make sure things are hung securely on the wall. Buy a fireproof safe box for important papers.

❑ Have wills and advance health care directives prepared for you and your wife. Give careful consideration to choosing a guardian for your children.

❑ Begin a retirement savings plan if you haven't already. Evaluate any plans at work and take advantage of matching money. Set up a regular, automatic contribution to make it easy.

❑ Begin a college savings program. Set up another regular, automatic contribution to make it easy. Remind family and friends how to write a check if they want to contribute as well.

Chapter 5

Preparing for the Big Day (or Night)

▶ No team heads to a championship game without a lot of preparation and a well thought out game plan. You and your wife shouldn't either. Delivery day is one of the most memorable events of your life. It requires preparation and lots of situational planning. Got a third down and fifteen yards to go? You know the play to call. Two hours from home when your wife goes into labor? You know what to do. All of this planning requires you to be present for team meetings. It also requires you to protect, provide, partner, and play. So roll up your sleeves, turn on your ears, and start building a delivery day playbook with your wife.

Birthing Classes

You and your wife will probably have decided early on the place and professional involvement you are going to have for your child's birth. With this the foundation of your birth plan is in place. Once the foundation is set, the next opportunity presented to many "first baby" couples is some type of birthing class. Your local hospital often hosts these. Check with your doctor and hospital for more information. If you have a different type of delivery planned check around and see what types of preparation classes are out there.

If you attend a traditional birthing class at a hospital, you should expect good overall information, covering what the experience will look like and feel like. Breathing, positioning, pushing, and how the father can help will all be included. You will probably get a tour of the facility including the rooms you will be in. If this is your first baby you should definitely enroll in one of these classes and learn as much as you can. Several other expectant couples will be there to form some comradery with as you all prepare for the big day together.

The good news is that hospitals are filled with great nurses and doctors who make a living delivering babies and dealing with rookie dads.

The deal with birthing classes is this: nothing can fully prepare you for the big day. Nothing. In the heat of battle you are going to forget much of what you learned. You will face circumstances never discussed. The good news is that hospitals are filled with great nurses and doctors who make a living delivering babies and dealing with rookie dads. They will be there to help, coach, and tell you what to do. They won't let you mess it up.

One thing you will want to know, class or no, is how to get to the hospital. You and your wife need to make a practice run to the venue of your delivery. Is there a special place for moms in labor to park? Do you know what floor or area of the hospital to go to when you are in labor? Sometimes minutes can make a difference. You don't want to be riding up and down elevators or circling the parking lot looking for the right spot when your big day finally arrives. Make sure your wife takes the practice run with you and knows where to go. You might not be the one who takes her to the hospital, so she will need to know the details.

Another item to take care of at the hospital ahead of time is preregistration. Most facilities will allow you to fill out the bulk of your admission and insurance paperwork ahead of time. There will still be a few things to complete when you arrive to have your baby, but you can knock out the majority ahead of time. You and your wife will have a less hectic day if you do.

Delivery Plays

You and your wife will want to be in step on several procedures before you hit the delivery room doors. Your doctor will be discussing the pros and cons of each with you and they will be covered in most birthing classes. Most are easy decisions. But BEFORE the big day you and your wife need to discuss each possible play and be in agreement on each. Your doctor and your own personal situation will dictate what specific things to discuss.

One of the big decisions is whether to use an epidural. The epidural is a method of delivering medication that will greatly decrease the pain in your wife's lower body during delivery. Your physician can discuss the pros and cons associated with using an epidural and delivering more naturally without one. Your wife may experience some desire or peer pressure to tough it out and go without an epidural. Your job is to help her hear the information, think through it, and come to a sound decision. Support her every step of the way.

If you decide as a couple to go natural, know it is no small commitment. You both have to be mentally tough. Your wife has to be in good shape and have a high tolerance for pain. Her concentration skills have to be strong. Your doctor and delivery team need to be in step with your commitment. Be cautious of "trying it without" and seeing how far you can go. There are points in the delivery process where it is simply too late to get an epidural going.

If you and your wife decide to go with an epidural don't feel like you are wimping out. Plenty of pain and work will still be involved in getting your bundle of joy out into the world. One recent study shows that more than 66 percent of babies born vaginally in the U.S. are now delivered with the assistance of an epidural.[6] Again, make your decision together and make sure your doctor is on board with it.

Other delivery plays you will want to discuss *well in advance of your due date* and be in agreement on include:

1. *Pitocin:* This and other drugs can be administered to help regulate contractions and get the delivery process moving. Your wife will get these through an IV. If you get bogged down in slow labor, Pitocin can help get it going. It can help keep your wife from becoming so exhausted before it is time to do the big pushing.

2. *Inducement:* If your wife doesn't go into labor on her own, some physicians will recommend inducing labor through drugs like Pitocin and other procedures. The is kind of like jump starting a car—once your wife's body gets going, it will take over and finish the process. Talk with your doctor about when he or she would recommend inducing. One advantage to inducing is knowing the exact day the baby will arrive.

3. *Episiotomy:* This is a cutting procedure the delivering physician will do to enlarge the birth canal if necessary. You probably won't have much of a choice in this. The alternative is tearing, which isn't much fun either. In either case your wife will be stitched back together and not suffer any long-term consequences. Talk with your doctor about when they recommend an episiotomy. The majority of women delivering their first child are likely to have a tear or an episiotomy.

4. *Forceps and suction:* These are tools the delivery team may use to help guide the baby through the last part of the birth canal. They are typically only used if the delivery process is bogged down and the baby isn't progressing through. They can often prevent the need for a C-section. Again, consult with your doctor on these before you hit the delivery room and make sure you are all in agreement.

5. *C-section or Cesarean section:* There are medical and non-medical reasons for delivering via C-section. About 30 percent of the babies born in the U.S. arrive this way for one reason or another. Most first time parents want to give regular vaginal birth a try. Talk with your physician about when they do C-sections. Listen to your wife's thoughts and concerns as well. You should both prepare yourselves for the possibility of C-section and know what is involved.

Post-Game Plays

Once your beautiful baby arrives you will have to run a few other big plays. Just like your delivery plays you will want to discuss these with clear heads well in advance of the big day. The two biggest decisions are whether to breast-feed and if you have a boy, whether to circumcise.

Breast-feeding is a big topic, no pun intended. While your wife has the deciding vote in this matter it is definitely something you need to discuss as a couple. You both need to be in agreement and you need to wholeheartedly support your wife on this topic.

There are several advantages to breast-feeding. This information is readily available from your pediatrician, your OB/GYN, and other sources. The bottom line is breast milk does a fantastic job of feeding your baby's body, brain, and immune system in the early months of life. Most new mothers at least give it a shot to see how it goes. Breast-feeding is a big job for your wife. Your job will be to support and encourage her—and to pick up the slack in other areas of baby and family care to help lighten the load. More on this later, soldier.

If you make the joint decision not to breast-feed, that is cool too. Feeding baby formula with a bottle definitely allows Dad to help more. It has been said there is no more noble a task in the world than pouring milk into babies. While most information shows some health advantages to breast milk, formula babies turn out fine as well. I know several babies who never had a drop of breast milk. They are intelligent, have strong immune systems and bodies, good math skills, no harmful addictions, and aren't in prison. As in breast-feeding, you need to talk about this as a couple, and you need to support your wife in the final decision.

> *It has been said there is no more noble a task in the world than pouring milk into babies.*

If you are having a boy, the other decision to discuss before delivery is circumcision. This is an individual decision for most couples. The majority of boys in the United States are circumcised, so your son may appreciate having it done when he hits the showers in junior high school. Another reason to circumcise may be religious preferences. Lastly there are some health reasons, especially that a circumcised penis is easier to keep clean. For some families it's an easy decision—they want Junior to look like dad in this area. Decide together.

Delivery Room Tone

Perhaps the most important pre-game discussion you can have with your wife is about the *tone* of the delivery room. Tone is a complex equation of people, noise, environment, cameras, phones, mood, and more. On one end of the scale your delivery tone can be an intimate and quiet experience with only you, your wife, and some medical personnel at the birth. On the other end you can have a Grand Central Station experience with a bleacher full of family and friends in the delivery room, multiple phones ringing off the hook, and the local newspaper snapping photos.

Whatever tone you select, it is your job, Dad, to manage it and make sure things don't get out of control. If you have always wanted to crank up the volume in your role as protector, then now is your chance. Here are some questions to discuss with your mate regarding the tone of your delivery:

- → Who do you want to allow in the delivery room prior to delivery?
- → Who do you want in the delivery room at the very moment of delivery?
- → What "view" do you want those present at delivery to have?
- → Do you want to take any phone calls while you are in the delivery room?
- → If you are taking calls, at what point in delivery do you say "no more"?
- → Do you want any other noise going in the room, including TV?
- → If you would like to have some background music playing, what specific artists and selections do you want?
- → How much photography and video do you want?
- → What lighting do you want in the room—high, low, or neutral?
- → Does your wife want a mirror available to watch the birth?
- → What other things would help you create the tone you want?

Whatever you and your wife decide on these items, remember this: delivery day is all about you and your baby and nobody else. If you really don't want Aunt Marge front row center for the final push, then politely tell her in advance. It is your job as Dad to make the experience what you and your wife want it to be.

Handling Advice

As a first time parent you will likely be besieged by advice from those who already have babies. While most experienced parents' wisdom is well intended, you still need to manage it or you could end up making some choices you aren't that crazy about. Some experienced parents are crazy in how they present to first time parents. They often present their birthing dogma as the ONLY way to go: You MUST deliver the baby into a pool of 72-degree water while standing on your head. You must only use Doctor So and So. You must only eat so and so.

Some would say the best advice is to not take any advice. I think a better approach is this: politely listen to it, process it, and then file it in your mind. You may file much of it in your mind's trashcan but you may also hear a few things that can help you. Listen and learn from those who have gone before you.

What you shouldn't do when someone gives you his or her angle is go away in a huff or pretend you aren't involved and it's all your wife's deal. Listen politely and then say something such as, "We will keep that in mind," "That sounds like something to consider," or even a simple, "Thank you."

The bottom line is you and your wife are creating your own experience with your own style and preferences. Advice from others can help, but it shouldn't consume you. This day belongs to you and your wife and nobody else.

Communication and Encouragement

During pregnancy your wife needs two things from you above all else: she needs you to listen to her and to talk to her. She needs you to really turn on the friend component of being a great husband. For example, if you are encountering some birthing dogma from the parent pros out there, she is getting it tenfold from her gang. She needs to talk through that stuff and more.

You need to ask your wife what her worries are and then really listen to her. The classic first time mom's worries often include these three:

1. Will I be a good mother?
2. Will our baby be healthy?
3. Will I ever get my "normal" body back?

After careful listening, this is the time when you can be a leader and help calm these fears and truly encourage your wife. Assure her that she will be a good mother. God has wired women to do this job and she will be wonderful at it. Remind her of the other life skills she may have that can apply: organization, a fun sense of humor, dedication, style—or whatever unique qualities she brings.

As far as a healthy baby, remind your wife the two of you need to continue to work hard and do everything in your power to help the equation. No smoking and no drinking or illegal drugs. She needs to follow your doctor's advice, eat right, take the proper vitamins, exercise, and get plenty of rest just to name a few. And she needs to *relax* and *enjoy* the whole experience. Lastly, remind her that more than 97 percent of all babies born in the United States have no birth defects.

The third big worry is body changes. The average weight gain in pregnancy for a woman of average height is twenty-five to thirty-five pounds. Your wife may need to gain more or less weight, depending on her weight before pregnancy and her health care provider's recommendations. In general most women will gain about two to four pounds during the first thirteen weeks of pregnancy and average one pound a week for the remainder of the pregnancy.

For most of your wife's adult life she has probably been trying to avoid any type of weight gain. Now the pounds are coming fast and furious. And while most women will acknowledge this is inevitable, they still don't want to gain "too much." My wife worried with each of our three pregnancies that she was going to set a new world record for weight gain. But when the dust settled she had gained around the same twenty-five pounds with each pregnancy.

Pregnancy is an awesome time and your wife looks more beautiful than ever. Remind her of that.

Your job on the weight gain topic is to encourage and support. Assure your wife she will get her pre-pregnancy body back, that she will lose the weight, and that you will be there to help and support her every step of the way. What you don't want to do is make fun of her gain or tell her you are worried about her getting the old body back. For example, my wife and I have some friends who went through their first pregnancy. During a gathering the new dad-to-be loudly proclaimed to his buddies (and within earshot of his wife and her friends) that his only hope was his wife would look as good after the baby arrived as she did before becoming pregnant. While his intentions may have been to be funny, it was still not cool. Don't put that kind of silly pressure on your spouse.

The bottom line is your wife is sacrificing her body to have your baby. You need to be thankful and supportive. A woman is never more feminine than when she is pregnant. It is an awesome time and your wife looks more beautiful than ever. Remind her of that. And while you are at it, remind all of your friends and family—when she is around—how beautiful she is pregnant. That is cool.

Finally, ask your wife what her dreams are for your family. Ask her what kind of home life she envisions, what activities she sees the family involved in, what schools and what neighborhood or community she would like to be a part of. Share some of your dreams with her. Don't make it an argument about money; this is dreamtime. Have fun with it. Play. Laugh, listen, talk, encourage, pray, and enjoy this fun time in life. Listen intently to her dreams and desires because it is your job, Prince Charming, to help make them come true.

Packing for the Hospital

One of the fun things to do during pregnancy is to pack your bag for the hospital. It is kind of the final checkpoint before you blast off into space and the great parenting unknown.

The key is to pack well in advance of your delivery day. Don't put it off thinking you can do it a few days (or minutes) before your scheduled date. Remember, even babies in the womb have minds of their own. They often decide when it is time to be born, not you or your doctor. This happened with our second child. We were cruising along comfortably three weeks before our due date when at midnight my wife's water broke. A few minutes later we were in the car and headed to the hospital. A few hours later we had a baby. That really wasn't our plan, but we were prepared and rolled with it.

You and your wife should each have a bag packed five weeks in advance of your due date, more if your doctor suggests the baby could come sooner. If there are items you are using in everyday life (toothbrush, deodorant) you don't want to pack as you go out the door then buy duplicates. You might not have much time to hunt those things down when your time comes. If you must have a last minute item to retrieve, then tie a note to your bag so you don't forget it. Place your "go bags" somewhere in the house so they can be easily remembered by you or found by a friend or family member.

You and your wife will undoubtedly have unique items to pack. Here are some things to consider taking along:

- ➝ *Your own PJs:* Most hospital gowns are not too flattering. Your wife may be much more comfortable in her own PJs in the days following delivery. You'll also be sleeping at the hospital, so take something appropriate for the public—like sweats—in case you need to make a 2:00 a.m. ice run down the hall.
- ➝ *Your own music:* We talked about delivery room tone. This will carry over to your post delivery room. Take some mellow tunes to play as background for you, your wife, your visitors, and your new baby to enjoy. Remember, no candles allowed at the hospital.
- ➝ *Clothes and personal items:* Think going away for the weekend. You will need some clothes and personal items such as deodorant and a toothbrush. Your wife will want to take her things too.
- ➝ *Cameras:* This might include a still-shot camera and a video camera. Remember to bring plenty of film, batteries, and the plug-in chargers. It is good to have two devices. In case one acts up you will still have a way to capture the moment for the ages.
- ➝ *Phones:* If you and your wife both have cell phones, bring them along with the plug-in chargers. You will be burning some minutes spreading the good word.
- ➝ *Pillow:* During pregnancy or before your wife may have found a favorite pillow. Take this along if it will help her

sleep. If you have a special linen spray at home bring some of that along as well to help make her hospital bed nicer.

→ *Baby's coming home outfit:* These are the clothes you will bring your baby home in. Your wife will undoubtedly be putting some thought into this and you should be involved. Make sure they are packed.

→ *Cash:* Make sure you show up at the hospital with some cash in your pocket. This isn't the mall. You may need some coin to get a cup of coffee or an emergency sandwich.

→ *Snacks:* Delivery can often take some time once you hit the hospital doors. While your wife won't be able to eat, you will and you should. A guy has to keep up his strength. Take some tidy snack food along like granola bars or fruit. Note that I said tidy. Don't take the Big Grab bag of Doritos. Not tidy, quiet, or cool.

→ *Notebook and pen:* A spiral notebook can be invaluable. It is a handy place to keep track of gifts you receive while at the hospital or to write down phone numbers or other information. Doctor care notes for Mom and Baby can also go in here. Should your wife or baby have any complications, you will see a sea of doctors and be presented with a lot of information. A notebook can help your and your wife's tired brains keep it all straight. Another option is to record everything in the Notes section of this book.

→ *Call lists:* You will want to call, text, or email friends and family when the big moment arrives. A list of people and numbers can help make sure you don't forget anyone. My wife and I had three lists: people to call while we were on our way to the hospital, people to call (if time) once we got settled in the delivery room, and people to call after the delivery. You should carry the load of switchboard operator. On your own special list to call include the name of a good flower shop. Find one that delivers fast and on the weekends.

- → *Sibling gifts:* If you have other children meeting their new sibling at the hospital, a gift exchange can help with the introductions. Help older brothers and sisters choose gifts for the new baby and wrap them ahead of time. Likewise, the new baby should have gifts wrapped the older kids will like. Good choices are movies, books, or games they can enjoy while the adults visit.
- → *This book:* Don't forget your trusty survival manual here! It has all of the phone numbers, schedules, questions, notes, lists, and other information you will want to have handy—not to mention it can provide some good reading during lulls in the action at the hospital.

Other To-dos

Before you head to the hospital with your wife in labor, you need to tackle another important project: purchase and install your new child's car seat. Many hospitals won't release you and your baby until they see a properly installed seat. This is not something you want to be doing for the first time in the hospital parking lot. You would think such a device wouldn't be that complicated, right? Think again.

There is a certain art to getting one of these things installed properly so it doesn't move. And it can take a little while the first time. So make sure the car seat is installed several weeks before you are due to deliver. Or practice it a few times and then keep the seat in the trunk of the car you will be coming home from the hospital in. It is a good idea to install the seat and then get an experienced mom or dad to check your work. Many police and fire departments are also willing to check your installation. Get that seat in there tight!

One last item you and your wife may want to carry in your cars is what I call the "water break repair kit." It is quite possible your wife's water could break (see definitions for water break) at any point late in pregnancy. And when it breaks it can break big. She won't be able to control the flood of fluid. Depending where she is, some clean up and a change of clothes might be in order—ala the water break repair kit. Keep a couple of old bath towels in your cars along with a change of clothes for her.

You can see that as your big day gets closer you and your wife need to be at the top of your game in communicating and partnering. There is plenty of game planning to do. There are lots of things to pack and square away at home before the big day. Make sure you are involved. Engage in the delivery process mentally and physically. Your 5 P jobs of being present, providing, protecting, partnering, and playing are in full gear at this point. And you are about to put the pedal to the metal and take it up even another notch.

As your big day gets closer you and your wife need to be at the top of your game in communicating and partnering.

FATHER, bless my wife and me with additional strength as we prepare to bring this baby into the world. Let those around us understand and appreciate this special time and what it means to our growing family. Bless us with excellent care and a healthy baby. Guide our choices and bless each decision. In the name of the Master Physician we pray, **AMEN.**

Wisdom to Consider

"The trouble with the world is not that people know too little, but that they know so many things that ain't so."

MARK TWAIN

"Be prepared."

BOY SCOUT MOTTO

Listen and learn. Absorb what works for you and your wife and filter out the rest. Communicate, plan, prepare, and have fun doing it!

☑ CHAPTER CHECKLIST

❑ Attend a good childbirth class at the hospital with your wife. Make it a priority on your schedule and go with a good attitude.

❑ Make a practice run to the hospital prior to week 32 in your pregnancy. Find out where to park and what floor to go to. Preregister for your upcoming delivery.

❑ Discuss delivery pain management in detail with your wife and your doctor. Have a clear understanding and plan for what you want and when.

❑ Talk about other delivery plays with your wife and your doctor. Cover Pitocin, inducement, episiotomy, forceps and suction, and C-section. Have basic agreement on each but understand the need to be flexible in the delivery room if new circumstances come up.

❑ Work with your wife on the decision to breast-feed or use formula. Make up your mind to assist as much as humanly possible with either method.

❑ If you are delivering a boy, decide whether to circumcise.

❑ Talk with your wife about the delivery room tone you both desire. Decide on who will be in the delivery room and when. Decide on camera and phone use. Decide on music, lighting, mirror use, and other items relevant to your situation.

❑ Prepare to manage the delivery room tone you and your wife decide on. This job is all you. It is part movie producer, part bouncer, and part administrative assistant. It is all husband.

❑ Handle baby advice from others with class. Listen and learn. Absorb what you like and quietly discard the rest. Build your own experience with your wife with the benefit of others' wisdom. Always thank others for their advice and ideas.

❑ Listen to your wife's concerns and offer constant encouragement. Think carefully and prepare ahead of time for your responses to the Big Three: "Will I be a good mother? Will our baby be healthy? Will I get my "normal" body back?"

❑ Ask your wife about her dreams for your new family. What does she want your family to stand for? What are her priorities and values? Where does she want to live? Share your dreams too. File it all in your mind and begin working on them. You must take the lead in making them come true.

❑ March through the packing list presented in the chapter. Have it all ready to go at least five weeks prior to your due date. Put each of your bags where a friend or family member could easily find them. Attach a reminder list of those last minute items to put in the bags.

❑ Purchase and install your baby's car seat before your wife goes into labor. Have your install job checked by another person in the know.

❑ Get your call lists together and go over them with your wife. Don't rely on numbers stored in your cell phone. Take a few minutes and put some key numbers in the back of this book or somewhere on paper. Remember a flower shop number.

❑ Hold hands with your wife and pray together. Pray for your baby, your wife, yourself, and your marriage. Thank God for the wonderful gift of a new baby.

Chapter 6

Delivery—Ready or Not, Here I Come!

▶ Your big day (or night) has finally arrived. The Super Bowl of marriage togetherness: bringing a new baby into the world. If you have been looking for some action and new experiences then you won't be disappointed with childbirth. Your 5 P skills will all be needed in a big way from here on out.

With the majority of babies in the U.S. being born in a hospital setting, this chapter will lean to that experience. If you are delivering at a birthing center, at home, in a taxi, or another non-hospital setting, you will need to adjust the material to your situation. It is still the same work and the same miracle—only the environment is different.

Like the famous philosopher Forrest Gump said, "Life is like a box of chocolates; you never know what you're gonna get" (1994, *Forrest Gump*, Paramount Pictures). So it goes with childbirth and the time leading up to it. Each labor and delivery has different speed, intensity, and circumstances.

Whatever circumstances come along your job as husband and coach is to be the calm encourager. Or at least try to be the calm encourager. Like that box of chocolates, your wife may go a number of different directions when the big day arrives. She may be calm and cool or she may rocket out of her mind into outer space. Or she might be somewhere in between the two. If she happens to go into outer space, your job is to be calmly present on Earth to provide, protect, partner, and play.

Landing at the Hospital

You will likely show up at the hospital with your wife in one of three stages: (1) with strong and steady contractions, (2) with a broken water membrane, (3) ready for a scheduled inducement.

Remember that once your wife is headed down the delivery track she shouldn't have anything to eat. If she has too much food in her stomach it can potentially cause problems. Follow your doctor's guidance here. You, on the other hand, need to eat. This is going to be a long day and you need to keep your focus. Take some snacks or buy some at the hospital. Ask the nursing staff about getting some chow to eat in or near your wife's room if you are involved in a long labor. The coach never leaves the stadium at halftime so don't you leave the hospital!

One of your first jobs at the hospital will be to check in and complete any remaining paperwork. Hopefully, you were able to preregister and knock out most of the forms. You will need to stow your overnight bags as well as get the items you want for delivery like cameras, music, phones, and so forth. Ask the nurses and hospital staff where you should put your gear. This isn't a hotel so don't be looking for a valet to handle this for you. Many hospitals do have luggage carts, so ask about one if you need it when you land or when you leave.

Next you will be getting to the room where you will deliver. The nursing staff will guide you and your wife through each step. If you have a written birthing plan or some specific things you want to occur, this is the time to ask the staff who it should be presented to. Even if your doctor is well aware of your preference, the staff probably is not. Be polite and respectful in your requests. Remember its okay to be firm, but also keep in mind you need to be flexible in your plans depending on the circumstances.

Part of your plan will consist of the "tone" you and your wife want the delivery to have. And you, big man, are the official Tone Manager and Protector. Remember the tone is made up mainly of the people, volume, and background noise of the delivery room. Cell phones, TV volume, and Aunt Marge all need to be under control. If you brought some relaxing music turn it on low and get settled.

The best thing you can do at the hospital, from the time you enter as two until you exit as three, is to encourage and honor your wife.

I remember for one of our deliveries my wife and I arrived at the hospital at 2:00 a.m. on the weekend. We were soon greeted quite loudly by my wife's brother and a gang of his friends who were just wrapping up a night on the town. Although my wife and I were excited about the delivery, our voices and spirits weren't quite as elevated as our visitors. The situation was politely managed and things returned more to the tone we wanted.

When you get to the hospital, you will want to call or text people and let them know what's going on. Be quick about it and keep the crowd present informed and under control.

The best thing you can do at the hospital, from the time you enter as two until you exit as three, is to encourage and honor your wife. She needs lots of encouraging words, handholding, and hugs. And you can honor her by cranking up the volume on your 5 P's. If you do all this everything else is going to take care of itself.

Labor and Delivery

The nursing staff will do most of the work leading up to the moments before delivery. If your physician is not present, the nursing staff will keep him or her up to date on your wife's progress. Many physicians will come in periodically to see you before pushing starts, while some will appear just in time to "catch" the baby. You will encounter other delivery staff including an anesthesia team if your wife is going to get an epidural or other pain management medications.

Regardless of the training, reading, classes, or previous experience you have with delivery, the hospital staff will guide you through all of it. Don't panic if you feel unprepared. They will not let you or your wife fail. If they tell you to hold a leg or change your breath counts—do it.

Don't panic if you feel unprepared. The hospital staff will not let you or your wife fail.

Early in the labor your wife may get some monitor hookups. These vary by hospital and physician but each is intended to monitor the health of your wife and baby. One will likely monitor your wife's contractions and another will monitor the baby's heartbeat. All are indicators for the staff to follow and a basis for decisions.

The first part of labor will be riding out the up-and-down waves of contractions. The contractions will increase in intensity and frequency as labor progresses. Your role as coach and encourager really gets turned on when it's time to manage contractions and later on with pushing.

The delivery team will also be checking your wife to see how far she is dilated and effaced. Dilation is measured on a scale of 1 to 10. Your wife will progress all the way up the dilation scale to 10, which is go time. Effacement is typically measured as a percentage.

Once the stars align and the staff sees the right mix of contractions, dilation, and effacement, they will call for your wife to begin pushing. This will involve your wife getting her body in the right position, pushing for a count, and then resting for a count. And dude she needs to hear *your* voice in those counts, so take the nurses' direction and get in there and count and encourage.

Much can be said about what to do and not do in the delivery room. A lot will depend on what circumstances you are in at delivery and what, if any, pain medications your wife is using. Here is a list of coaching do's and don'ts that should be widely applicable:

- →ı DO listen to the delivery team and their instructions.
- →ı DON'T tell your wife this baby thing was all her idea anyway.
- →ı DO constantly encourage your wife; let her hear your voice.
- →ı DON'T let her be discouraged if things go slowly.
- →ı DO be her advocate and tell the staff what she needs or wants.
- →ı DON'T let another relative slide in as head coach. That's your job!
- →ı DO be an advocate of managing your wife's pain and comfort.
- →ı DON'T tell your wife she is a wimp or not strong.
- →ı DO pray with your wife. Pray for strength and a healthy baby.
- →ı DON'T become a patient yourself. Sit down or get a drink of water.
- →ı DO take some tasteful photos and video during labor.

Stay in the Game

The time it takes getting to the point where the baby starts to appear can vary. Some labors are short, perhaps a couple of hours with only a few minutes of pushing. Others can be quite long, with more than twenty-four hours of pushing.

Remember your wife is the athlete in the arena. She is going to invest every last ounce of energy she has and then some. If she gets mentally or physically fatigued, your job is to keep a steady handle and encourage her back to the task at hand. If the pain seems unbearable to her, keep encouraging. Remind her the pain will be gone soon. Focus thoughts on the baby and how awesome it will be to meet him or her. If your wife gets totally exhausted, tell the staff your thoughts and regroup. Nobody knows your spouse better than you so be her advocate.

Watching your baby wiggle its way into the world is the most magical of moments. . . . It is one that will inspire and encourage you the rest of your life.

Don't forget about managing the delivery room tone. Control the number of visitors, the number of phone conversations, and all the other distractions around you. Keep the tunes going if your wife likes to have music in the background.

If necessary remind the delivery staff of some of the delivery room plays you and your wife previously discussed. This would include forceps, suction, episiotomy, C-sections, and others. None of these may even be necessary but at least you will have them out on the table.

The final stage of delivery is absolutely the best. The baby's head has crowned (appeared) and the doctor and staff are all in position. The team will coach you and your wife through the final pushes. If you are holding one of your wife's legs you will have a great view of a new life coming into the world. If your wife wants to view the delivery many rooms are set up with a mirror for her to watch.

Watching your baby wiggle its way into the world is the most magical of moments. It is one God smiles openly upon—and you can feel it. Take that magical moment and imprint it in your mind. It is one that will inspire and encourage you the rest of your life.

Houston, We Have a Baby!

Your baby has arrived! One of the first things that will happen is the doctor will announce whether it is a boy or a girl. This may not be new information if you found out the sex during an ultrasound, but at least you will learn if it was correct. Nearly every parent does a quick count of fingers, toes, ears, and other body parts.

At this point you need to hug your wife and congratulate her with a kiss. And you should give her a huge, sincere THANK YOU for all of her effort and hard work during delivery. She has sacrificed her body for the delivery and she needs to hear your gratitude.

Most birth teams want to get Baby to Mom as soon as possible, but there is some business and clean up to take care of. The umbilical cord must be cut and the father is usually given the option to do this. Follow the staff's instructions and do it! You will be so glad you did.

Make sure you have your cameras ready during those moments immediately following delivery, but be careful. Your wife may not be in a position of modesty. I have accidentally shot some not so family friendly video of my wife right after delivery, so be aware of what you capture on the screen!

Right after birth the physician and staff will give your baby an overall health assessment. They will clean the baby's airways if necessary and give an APGAR test to grade his or her condition. The baby will also likely get an antibiotic ointment in the eyes. Expect your new arrival to be weighed, measured, cleaned, diapered, banded with identification, wrapped, and handed to Mom.

Don't expect your baby to look like that plump little one on the Gerber food jars right away. Being born is a rough ride. But they will still be the most beautiful baby you have ever seen.

The first looks into each other eyes are another special moment when Mom and Dad finally get to meet Baby. This is the project you have been talking about and feeling for months. And now you finally get to SEE that bundle of joy. Enjoy these moments as they are among life's finest.

You now have another human being you must be present for, provide for, protect, partner with, and play with. Your to do list just got a whole lot longer for the rest of your life.

Managing Your Stay

If you have a crowd waiting outside for the arrival, they will likely be anxious to see you once the delivery room is cleared and your wife is ready for them. In some hospitals you will finish your stay in the room where you delivered while in others you will be moved to a different room for the duration. If you move, your job is to tote any necessary gear to the new spot.

One thing you need to do immediately is order some flowers for your wife and have them delivered to your room ASAP. This is mandatory! Your wife just birthed your child, which is no small feat, and flowers are the universal sign of appreciation and love. If you got her a special gift for the moment (remember no appliances or cash) the first hours after birth is a great time to give it to her. Your overall mission is to thank her and show your appreciation for what she has done the past nine months and today.

Your role of patient advocate is critically important now. Be vigilant and present for your wife's recovery. Talk to her about how she is feeling. Help her work with the nursing staff in managing her pain and her recovery. When it is time for her to use the toilet for the first time following delivery, you need to be there for support. When she needs to get up and walk, you need to be the one holding her hand and encouraging her.

When the love of your life needs something to eat or drink work with the hospital staff to get it or go find it and bring it in. If she really has a craving for a special something (ice cream, steak, corn dog, Starbucks, or whatever) it is your job to make it happen. But don't take that as a license to hop in your car and drive across town for half a day to get something. Your job is to stay at her side. Use your network of family and friends on the outside world to bring something in if necessary. Most people love to help in this fun kind of way.

Your role of patient advocate is critically important now. Be vigilant and present for your wife's recovery.

Another key job during your stay will be visitor management. A certain segment of friends and family likely will want to visit with you and your new baby in the first day or two after delivery. These should be visits you and your wife enjoy with some of the most important people in your life, but they should happen on your schedule. Here are ten tips on directing the flow of visitors and well wishers:

1. Get the word out via phone, text, email, and word of mouth that ALL prospective visitors should call before they come to make sure the time is good.
2. If you can't get a bunch of calls or messages out, work with a friend or family member to put the word out to a list you give them.
3. If you are using a cell phone to manage traffic, set it on vibrate and keep it in your pocket. That way your cool new ring tone won't wake your wife when she is resting.
4. Try to arrange a couple of blocks of time for visitors. One in the afternoon and one in the evening, to accommodate those people getting off work, can be good.
5. Try to schedule visitors around the times when your wife is resting, eating, and getting instructional or breast-feeding time with the baby.
6. Try to schedule any awkward or volatile family pairings at separate times. If it doesn't work out that way those

involved will just have to get over it. This day is about you and not them.

7. When your wife is resting during the day put a "Mother Resting" sign on the door of your room. Put a note on the sign for visitors to come back later and to call you to make sure it is a good time.

8. The hospital staff can also help you manage the flow of visitors. If it is rest time, make sure you tell them you aren't accepting any visitors for a certain amount of time.

9. Grandparents of the new arrival should get some special quiet time with the baby. If you can, try to arrange a visit from them when nobody else is visiting.

10. If your new baby has older siblings visiting, do the sibling gift exchange.

Making sure your spouse gets some rest is important. Delivery is like a marathon and her body needs to recover. So use the nursery and nursing staff to handle the baby for some periods of rest. Don't worry; they are professionals. You will have this youngster at home for the next twenty-plus years so a few hours in the nursery won't damage your relationship.

You can do several other little things to help your wife rest. For example, don't even think about sleeping in her hospital bed with her. She needs some room to get comfortable and that doesn't include you. Also no watching TV late into the night or playing video games. Leave your GameCube and Xbox at home. Take phone calls out of the room if she is sleeping. And you need to be getting some rest yourself, big fella. Take some time just to be still while at the hospital and prepare yourself for the work ahead.

Record Keeper

As mentioned earlier you will want something to keep track of any gifts visitors bring. This book has note pages designed just for this, or you can use a notebook. Both you and your wife will be fatigued and it will be hard to remember who brought what when it comes time to send thank-you notes. You may also want to send a note to those special people who took the time out to visit in person.

You will also want to write down any doctor notes or to do's for your wife and the baby. You may encounter some specialist physicians and you will want to get their names for future reference. Your notes can be invaluable down the road when you go to follow-up visits with doctors. Keeping good records now will make your life a lot easier later.

> *You need to be getting some rest yourself .... Take some time just to be still while at the hospital and prepare yourself for the work ahead.*

Don't Forgets

Throughout your stay you should keep up the role of chief photographer and historian. You will want to get plenty of still shots and video of Baby with Mom and key visitors like grandparents. Make sure you get in a few of the pictures yourself! If you can you may want to send a quick picture via email or your phone to family and friends. People love to get a picture of a newborn on their first day in the world.

Your wife and your baby will likely have more tests and exams before you leave the hospital. Make sure you are present for these or that you are made aware of the results. Write down any notes, physician names, or recommended follow-up care.

You will also likely have the opportunity to apply for your child's birth certificate, so if possible make sure you get that handled before leaving the hospital. Other options you may be given are to have a birth announcement in the local paper and to have your baby's picture professionally taken at the hospital.

Preparing to Go Home

If you have a traditional hospital delivery, at some point you will come to "going home day." You and your wife may feel a mix of emotions at this point. You may feel scared to leave the hospital walls with its staff of professional baby caregivers and delivered meals. You may also feel anxious to get home and dive into the next chapter of your lives. Whatever your emotions and energy level, know that you still need to be on your 5 P post and vigilant as you prepare to head through the doors.

Pay attention to the final doctor directives you get before discharge. Mom will have some and so will the new baby. Make sure you are present with your wife so you can both hear these. Write them down. Make sure you record follow-up appointments if they are set for you. If you need to call and schedule these when you get home, make yourself a reminder note. Get any necessary prescriptions before you leave and understand when and how the medicine should be taken.

Be sure to have that car seat installed and ready to go. Hopefully this is something you did ahead of time. It's no fun to agonize over a car seat for the first time in the hospital parking lot while your wife and baby are waiting on you. Double check your installation and make sure that thing is in there tight. Then install your baby in it with confidence.

By the way, driving for the first time with your new infant in the car can be a little nerve racking. It's a little like having a million-dollar crystal chandelier in the back seat. Since you can't take them home in an armored truck just relax, keep your eyes on the road (not on Baby), and take your time. You will get comfortable with "baby on board" soon enough.

Another nice goal: strive to arrive with your newly expanded family to a clean and organized home. The goal here for you and your wife is low stress upon entry—and a steaming pile of laundry and dirty dishes won't help. Things don't need to be Martha Stewart perfect but some general order can go a long way in that first day back. This might be a place where some friends and family could help if your house was in a bit of disarray when you left. Or if you are able to be gone from the hospital for a couple of hours while your wife rests, you could go pull the house together and then hurry back to your post. Approach it as if you won't be able to do anything but tend to your wife and baby for the first two days back home. Get the place together and lay in a few necessary groceries.

You will find this new chamber in your heart you never knew you had. It just opens up when you see your new baby.

Here are a few other last minute things to do before leaving the hospital:

- Make sure your thank-you list for gifts and visitors is complete.
- Get a "new baby" yard or door sign.
- Thank the staff for their help and guidance.
- Complete any final insurance or other paperwork.
- Get a luggage cart to load up your gear.

Wherever you deliver your baby or with whatever assistance you deliver, the result is the same: your life has changed forever. It is no longer just you and your wife. You are now a triad. All of the dynamics of life and marriage have changed. The good news is life should be even better and more complete than before. You will find this new chamber in your heart you never knew you had. It just opens up when you see your new baby. It doesn't get any better than this. Enjoy it and prepare yourself for the work ahead.

FATHER, give us strength, energy, and focus as we bring this baby into Your world. Bless this child with great health and wisdom from the first day of their life through their last. Bless my wife with a great delivery and recovery. Thank You, Lord, for this glorious event and impress it upon our minds as a lasting and energizing memory. In the name of the Great Physician we pray, **AMEN.**

Wisdom to Consider

"Anyone who thinks women
are the weaker sex has never
witnessed childbirth."

ANONYMOUS

You need to serve your wife on this day more than any other. She is sacrificing her body to make this play. Be present, provide, protect, partner, and play (have fun), and everyone will be fine.

☑ CHAPTER CHECKLIST

❑ Remind your wife not to eat after she goes into labor. Remember to take some snacks so you can eat and keep up your strength.

❑ Be in charge of any necessary paperwork when you arrive at the hospital. Take care of handling your luggage.

❑ Take the lead in helping your wife present your preferences and/or birthing plan to the hospital staff.

❑ Manage the tone of your delivery room. This includes people, phones, mood, and other intrusions.

❑ Be the phone screener for your wife if she is able to take calls. There may be people you want to keep updated, but this should be your job.

❑ Honor your wife! Encourage her, hold her hand, and give her multiple hugs.

❑ Listen to the delivery team and their instructions. Be a help wherever and whenever you can.

❑ Be an advocate for your wife. If she needs something make it known. Be a calm encourager and a good coach.

❑ Pray with your wife during delivery. If you are unsure what to say, use the prayer at the end of this chapter.

❑ Be a good cameraman. Take some good still photos and video during labor and once the baby arrives. These might be the most cherished photos you take your entire life.

❑ Thank your wife for a beautiful baby (say "thank you") and congratulate her.

❏ Get some flowers ordered ASAP once the baby arrives. These need to get to your wife within hours, not days, of delivery. If you have another special gift, present it as well.

❏ Be present and vigilant for your wife and your baby in the hours and days following delivery. Work with the hospital staff to make sure both have what they need. Make sure your wife has something she likes to eat.

❏ Manage the flow of visitors once the baby arrives. Make sure you and your wife have some "no visitor" time, so you can get some rest and have time just one on one—or now one-on-one-on-one time.

❏ Be the good news reporter. Get some phone calls, text, or emails out to key people who can help spread the word. Typical baby stats people want are date and time of birth, length, weight, and name. Let them know everyone is in good health as well.

❏ Keep track of gifts and visitors in this book or your notebook. You will need this to send thank-you notes later. Also record physician names and directives they give for your wife and baby.

❏ Install your new baby's car seat BEFORE you get to the hospital. Have it double-checked by another parenting pro or by someone else in the know.

❏ Arrange to have your house "together" when you and your wife return with the new baby.

❏ Complete any final paperwork before leaving the hospital including birth certificate applications, birth announcement, insurance billing, and son on.

Chapter 7

The First Forty Days and Nights at Home

▶ You and your wife have safely brought your new baby home and walked through the front door of the rest of your lives. Now what do you do? If you are asking this what to do question aloud or to yourself, the answer is very simple: you (Dad) do a lot!

This chapter will help guide you through those first forty days and nights in the wilderness—or being at home with a new baby. Forty days is significant as it equates to roughly the six-weeks mark. It is a crucial time when routines and roles are established. This is also when your wife may be considering a return to work outside of the home if that is your plan.

A sure way for the new father to organize himself in this busy time is around the 5 P model: be present, protect, provide, partner, and play. Let's take a look at each in these crucial first weeks at home with a new baby and a new mom.

Present and Accounted For

Throughout this book we have emphasized the importance of being physically and mentally present for your wife and children. Being present remains a key to success in these early days at home.

You must be present physically to help with the many tasks at hand: feeding, diapering, bathing, cooking, cleaning, and all of the other duties that go along with a new baby in the house. Remember the earlier discussion of getting your hands in the game?

Being present remains a key to success in these early days at home.

You must be present mentally for your wife and baby. You need to be watchful and observant of the health of both. You and your wife need to be sharing advice and opinions about what is going on with the baby. You need to have some thoughts on what works and what doesn't. Be a listener. Be an idea guy. Be an encourager. Remember the earlier discussion of getting your head in the game?

Be available to your wife twenty-four hours a day these first forty days. That doesn't necessarily mean you are physically by her side every minute of every day. She won't want you to be hovering that much. But when away from home you need to be reachable by phone for consult or support or even to share a fun moment. When you are together be ready to jump in and help when she asks. The baby is a top priority right now and you need to act accordingly.

If you have taken some days off for the birth you will need to eventually get back to work. If you have enough time built up you might consider taking off some half days in those first few weeks the baby is home. This could help give your wife some extra rest if needed or allow her to emerge into the outside world by herself while you handle baby duty. Keep plugged into your wife's mood and energy. If it seems like she needs a break, take some time off work and give her some time off.

Just like during pregnancy you need to attend key medical checkups with Mom and Baby. Mom will likely have a six-week appointment with her OB/GYN. You need to be there and help make sure her physical and emotional health are where they should be. Your baby will probably have two and four-week checkups or as directed by your pediatrician. You need to be present at those as well, listening to the doctor and offering your observations. Write questions and take notes in your book if necessary.

Life is forever changed when you bring a baby home. You must accept this. Don't expect an immediate return to your old routines. Be patient and flexible. Some things will get back to the way they were, but know that life is different now. The good news is life is better now! God gives us children as a gift to care for and as a way for us to grow closer to Him. Enjoy being present.

Protector and Deflector

Your role as protector continues when you land at home with a new baby. You can best guard your wife physically by making sure she isn't trying to do too much in those first forty days at home. Women's bodies are miraculous in what they can do. But childbirth still requires some healing time whether your wife had a vaginal birth or a C-section. You can help by encouraging her to rest and to follow her doctor's advice for recovery. Just helping her retrieve things around the house or taking things up and down the stairs can make a difference. This isn't the time for your wife to be splitting firewood in the backyard, so make sure you help with the lifting chores around the house for a while.

People love new babies and they will love yours. That means you may draw some crowds in those first days at home. Be agreed with your wife on who is coming over and when. Be careful not to say, "Come over anytime" because some people will take you up on the "anytime" part. You and your wife are going to be tired and adjusting to your new life. So you probably don't want to have a big wine and cheese party kicking off at 8:00 p.m. like you did in the "old days." Remember it is okay to say no or to reschedule visitors.

You will want to be protective of your commitments outside the house as well, including those at work. You won't want to take your newborn into big crowd situations in those first few weeks.

Be there for your wife if she encounters some of these ups and downs. Be part of the solution and not part of the problem.

Remember your new team of three isn't going to be as agile and flexible as your old team of two. Reserve the right to go back home at any point during those early trips into the outside world.

Another good protection plan is to make sure you are talking and listening to your wife about how she is feeling both mentally and physically. I mean *really talking and really listening*—the kind where you are looking into her eyes and you aren't distracted by anything else. The load of pregnancy, delivery, and being a new mom is a big one. You need to be there every step of the way, listening, encouraging, helping, and offering input as needed while her mind and body recover.

We will talk in detail in the next chapter about postpartum depression and the baby blues. For now just know that having a baby can create real spikes in female hormones and emotions. You need to be there for your wife if she encounters some of these ups and downs. Be part of the solution and not part of the problem.

Speaking of emotions, you need to be aware of your own. It is quite possible that with a little less sleep and more on your to do plate you could ride the emotional roller coaster too. Jealousy, fear, or anger can begin to appear for some men. While emotions are a natural response to our surroundings, don't let them manage your life. You manage them. If you are feeling some jealousy with the new baby, get in there and help and spend more time with your little one. If something upsets you with your wife, try giving it a day to rest. If it is still important to you the next day, then have an adult conversation about it. Ninety percent of the time it probably won't be important the next day.

During these first weeks at home your sex life will also be on hold. Your wife's doctor (and your wife) will tell you when it is physically okay for a return to a regular sex life. But also make sure your wife is mentally ready for it and you aren't pushing the issue too hard. You will both be a lot happier if you ease back into it and not rush it. Also remember as a couple you can be extra fertile during this time, so take that into careful consideration.

Here are some additional do's and don'ts in your role as protector:

- → DO feed your baby whenever he or she wants in the first few weeks—don't try to "stretch" them in between feedings.
- → DON'T let your newborn sleep through the night until given clearance by your doctor. Babies need to be fed at night, especially in the first two weeks at home.
- → DO trust your instincts and your wife's instincts when it comes to your baby's health, behavior, wants and needs.
- → DON'T take your newborn out into big crowds. It isn't healthy or safe with a just developing immune system.
- → DO get the baby and your wife out of the house, just not into a big crowd. Go for walks in the neighborhood or tackle the grocery store for a few items.
- → DON'T even think about smoking in the house with a newborn or allowing others to do so.
- → DO make sure your baby is sleeping on his or her back and not on the stomach.

→ DON'T pick up your baby at the very first cry or grunt during sleep. It is a natural part of the sleep cycle to make noise.
→ DO have your baby vaccinated.
→ DO have ANY fever in your newborn evaluated by a physician.

The last item regarding fever is one of which to be especially aware. A newborn baby should not have a fever, and if he or she does, your doctor needs to know about it right away. My wife and I gained firsthand knowledge of this the hard way.

With a new baby in the house you need to bring your A-game in love and leadership.

When our third child was one month old she suddenly quit eating and began to feel warm with a fever. Because we had other children, we were used to an occasional spike in temperature or an off day with them. But our instincts (especially my wife's) reminded us this was a newborn and that any fever needs attention.

Of course this occurred in the middle of a weekend when our pediatrician's office was closed. Knowing this couldn't wait until Monday, we called our pediatrician's on-call nurse and she guided us through getting an accurate rectal temperature. That temperature reading was high enough to earn us an immediate trip to the hospital emergency room and a two-week hospital stay. Our daughter is fine today, but we did end up with a diagnosis from that initial fever that required a good bit of treatment and follow-up care.

The bottom line is ask your pediatrician what the guidelines are for fevers and calling in. It will probably be something such as anything higher than 100 degrees in the first six months needs a call. Never give your newborn any medication, including pain relievers like Tylenol and Ibuprofen, without consulting your pediatrician! Write your doctor's fever guidelines down and trust your instincts—and your wife's—if something doesn't feel right.

Provider Extraordinaire

With a new baby at home it is a good time to review the material covered earlier in the book. You will want to make sure your head, hands, and wallet are all in the game. Look hard at those chapter checklists and get caught up on all your to do's.

Remember the discussion about providing and what it means today? Not long ago a father could earn an *A* for providing income for a home and food on the table. Income, home, and food are still absolute priorities on your to do list. But you will remember that today's provider also has two *L* words to work on in this category: love and leadership. And with a new baby in the house you need to bring your A-game in love and leadership.

Recall our magic love formula. Providing unconditional love for your wife creates security in her. Her security leads to confidence, and her confidence leads to energy and enthusiasm. The marriage, the husband, and the baby all benefit from this super loved woman!

So how does one provide extra love in these crazy times? Every guy has his own way of doing this. We have also touched on several ideas throughout this book to help get you going. Just remember to be patient and encouraging. Find the humor in the moments where you are both learning to parent. Give some hugs. Tell your wife how much you love her. Tell her how much fun you are having being a dad and that you wouldn't want to do it with anyone but her. You get the picture.

The first forty days at home are the time to let those pent up leadership skills loose. Remember this is not the let-ME-tell-

YOU-what-to-do kind of leadership. That was clearing Aunt Marge out of the delivery room. This is the lead-by-example kind of leadership.

In this category you can put all random acts of kindness and all planned chores. You are providing the kind of leadership your wife truly appreciates when you help with some of the day-to-day household tasks. We will provide specifics in the partnering section in a moment. You can also refer to earlier chapters for ideas. The point is that once a new baby lands everyone has more to do. Lead by pulling as much of the load onto your shoulders as possible.

People instinctively want to help a couple with a new baby, so don't deny them the gift of giving.

One area you can assist with in the first weeks at home is steering offers for help. Family, friends, neighbors, church members, and others may offer. A common form of help in our culture is food. And because meal preparation takes time, what a great assistance this can be in the first weeks. Your wife won't have a lot of extra capacity, and you will have your hands full with your extra duties and your regular day job.

The key to meal management is to have a couple of days that would work for you and your wife to have a meal brought in. Often there will be enough to live on for at least two evening meals. Get a calendar and write in who is coming when. You should always offer as well for the giver to come anytime with a meal ready to freeze. People instinctively want to help a couple with a new baby, so don't deny them the gift of giving. Remember to put these gifts on your thank-you list to let the giver know it was greatly appreciated.

Another area you will want to work closely with your wife on is the hands on assistance from the baby's grandparents or other close relatives. This can range from being nonexistent to Grandma moving in for a couple of weeks or more. The comfort in your relationships with the new grandparents will also be all over the board. You and your wife might be excited about this help, or you might be dreading it. The best thing you can do is communicate through all of it. You and your wife should be together on what is acceptable to both of you. And you need to communicate with the well-intended family member. Use your leadership skills to make sure the situation doesn't become a big source of stress in the house. Enough said.

The other area to continue leading in is healthy lifestyle choices. You are going to need all the energy and focus you can muster. Support your wife in her choices as well. Help her get back into exercising when she is ready. Make sure you have good food choices available. Keep smoke and alcohol out of the house. Talk to her about her goals in these first weeks at home and be a part of that plan.

Be sure to take a leadership role in the spirituality of your home. Earlier in the book we discussed the strength that comes from you and your wife praying together. Continue to work in that direction, even if you just take baby steps at the dinner table. Pray for your marriage and for each other. Pray that you grow in your parenting skills. And pray for the healthy development and safety of your baby. If you aren't praying hard for your baby every day, who is? For more specific ideas, check out the Power Module in this book on How to Pray for Your Baby.

Lastly, get connected with your church and attend. If you don't have a church, then shop around and find one you and your wife like and go.

Howdee Partner

The partner *P* is where all the hard work and heavy lifting are found. You will be working (partnering) with your wife to get everything done that needs to be done. And with a new baby the list can get long and tiresome. One way to organize yourself is to break down what needs to be done into three categories:

1. Household tasks: meals, shopping, laundry, bill paying, etc.
2. Baby physical tasks: feeding, bathing, diaper changing, etc.
3. Family decision tasks: schedules, health decisions, etc.

This is a great time to sit down (or collapse on the couch) again with your wife and work out a basic plan. Understand (listen to) what she has on her plate each day and in the weeks ahead. Ask her how you can help. If she doesn't have any immediate input have some suggestions ready. Dishwasher duty? I'm all over it. Sunday night dinner—with enough leftover for Monday? I'm on it. Bathrooms cleaned? Yuck. But, I got it.

Reviewing Chapter 3, Getting Your Hands in the Game, will give you some ideas to keep you busy. There should be lots of opportunity for you to help with cooking, cleaning, laundry, shopping, bill paying, errand running, caring for pets, maintaining your home, and the other chores in your life.

Pay particular attention to those little things that can be stressors. For example, keep light bulbs replaced or fix the leaky faucet that drives everyone crazy. Take an objective look around. I mean really look around. If you stepped over a pile of laundry to get in the door, that might be a place to start. If you don't see anything, ask your wife what needs to be done. For example, there should be plenty of thank-you notes to log in and get out the door. You can always start working on writing those and/or addressing the envelopes.

Remember your wife may feel some pull to do it all: the baby, the house, the husband, and the world. Assure her she still has PLENTY on her plate. You are there to help her carry the load and take some of those sharp corners off that can lead to stress on a bad day. You aren't suggesting she quit doing everything that was once her domain. Some of those things she considers her job and she won't want to quit them. Just like you wouldn't quit doing certain things at your job you know are crucial to your success.

Hear this: you must not be paralyzed by these crazy, mixed-up times. There is no perfect time or circumstance to get involved; you must jump in and partner now! Above all, remember you aren't surrendering your manhood if you cook, clean, and change a diaper. A real man secures his marriage, family, and home by leading and getting things done, whatever the task.

Get assignments BEFORE you both go to bed, so each of you knows what to expect.

Work with Us

After you get a to do list for your household duties, it is time to move on to how you can help with baby related tasks. This is the fun part. And there is plenty to do: holding, soothing, feeding, diapering, bathing, dressing, loving, and more.

You will have baby tasks you and your wife share as they come up. I will do the bath tonight, or I will do this diaper change. Impromptu, on-the-spot task sharing and volunteering is a beautiful thing. There will also be some baby things you may want as a more regular assignment.

One example is nighttime feeding. If your wife is breast-feeding, you can still help out. For that middle of the night feeding you can go get the baby, change the diaper, and deliver him or her to Mom "ready to go." Some of the biggest stress in new parents can come in the middle of the night as each waits for the other to make a move when the baby wakes up. Get assignments BEFORE you both go to bed, so each of you knows what to expect. If your baby is bottle-feeding, then Dad can do an even more complete shift. As mentioned earlier a great way to partner on this is to play "zone." For example, Mom has all the wakeup calls from midnight to 4:00 a.m., and then Dad takes it from 4:00 a.m. until 8:00 a.m. Then each parent gets better sleep with a block of hours when they know they are off duty. Adjust the times to what works best for you and your wife. Above all, make sure you are doing your fair share.

Nighttime feeding is just one example of getting a firm assignment. The point is to eliminate the stress about whose turn it is to do something—whether feeding, bathing, diaper changing, or whatever. Talk it out and get a plan. And don't be afraid to change, adjust, and adapt along the way. Be flexible.

With a new baby in the house you can't sit on the bench. I know one husband who chooses not to be involved with the couple's children until about age two because that is the age he "really starts to like to play with them." That is so wrong and such a loss for everyone involved.

Just as sad is another couple where the wife won't allow her husband to help because "he doesn't know what he is doing." That is a fifteen-yard penalty on the wife and another fifteen yards on the husband. Make sure you become a student of this life phase and learn. Don't be afraid to jump in and try things. Learn from your wife and others around you. Read books. Learn what your baby's different cries sound like and what they mean. Learn your baby's bedtime routine. Learn how to calm them. Learn how to do a quick diaper change. The list goes on, but you get the point.

Check out the Power Module section of this book for some basic how to baby skills. You will find twenty topics covered, such as feeding, bathing, burping, diapering, swaddling, and calming a crying baby. You will even find pointers on how to quickly clean a house and how to build killer lasagna.

Two Heads

The old saying that two heads are better than one definitely applies to parenting a newborn. God designed it that way for a reason. You and your wife will need all the mental muscle you can muster.

Just like the physical tasks of parenting, make sure you are involved in the decision-making regarding your baby. Note I didn't say *make* all the decisions; I said to *be involved*—to collaborate and discuss things with your wife.

Make sure you become a student of this life phase and learn. Don't be afraid to jump in and try things.

For example, you will want to be involved when you decide where the baby will sleep during the first few weeks at home, especially at night. In the nursery? In a crib or bassinet in your room? You will also be faced with the decision of allowing the baby to sleep with you and your wife in your bed. Most medical professionals discourage this "co-sleeping" as it can be dangerous if you were to unconsciously roll onto the baby. And it can be a hard habit to break—trust me. But sometimes it is the only thing that allows everyone in the house to get some sleep. The point is, discuss and conquer.

Another example you may need to put your heads together on is sibling interaction with the new baby. If you have other children in the house, how are you training them to handle the baby? Are you and your wife consistent on what goes and what doesn't go? Again, work through the details as a parenting team.

Lastly, continue to guard your partner so she has the energy and strength to be a good decision maker and teammate. If she needs your help as a manager/agent, as discussed earlier in the book, then continue in that role as necessary. Above all continue to encourage each other. Tell each other that you both are doing a good job and making progress. There is a light (and more sleep) at the end of this forty-day tunnel.

Play Time

Our fifth and final *P* stands for play. Many other words could describe play, including relaxing, kicking back, down time, interacting, laughing, family time, healing, rejuvenating, alone time, working out, dating, and more. This is the time when the pressure is off and the fun is on.

In your life right now, three people really need you to help them have fun and play; your crazy new baby, your stressed wife, and your own bad self. Let's take a look at what you can do to help put some fun into each.

Did You See That?

Playing with your baby in the first few weeks of life is an awesome experience. No, you won't be building any tree houses or having tea parties together. But you do get to be a star for a few seconds or a few minutes at a time. You see, playing for your baby during these weeks will really just be them watching and listening to you.

In the early weeks your baby is starting to get in touch with the senses of sight, sound, and touch. He or she is also starting to learn they have arms, legs, and a head that move. Your role in playing is to help bring those senses and movements to life. So bring out your best comedy and dance material.

One simple thing you can do when your baby is awake is to talk to them. You finally have the undivided attention of someone to hear your best jokes and your life story! Babies want to hear your voice and observe how you make sound. In addition to regular conversation, babies love to hear you sing. Even if you are bad it doesn't matter. Something about music and melodies pleases even the youngest minds.

Another great play option at this age is reading. While your baby isn't going to be helping you turn the pages, he or she will start to recognize that books are objects of interest and they seem to make you talk. It is never too early to start building a love for reading in your little one.

It is never too early to start building a love for reading in your little one.

Remember not to engage your baby too much at night with reading aloud and talking. They need to learn these special treats are reserved for daytime and that nighttime is a quiet time for sleep.

Babies like to see you. Remember the part about being present? It starts here. Babies love to see you move your own arms and legs. They like to see your expressions. At some point they will mimic some of your movements.

It's always fun to unwrap your newborn to lay on a blanket and kick, stretch, and move. Get down close where they can see you and encourage everything they do. Move around some so they can learn to follow you with their eyes. Let them touch you or grip your fingers. Show them your best daddy dance moves. Now you are playing! Check out the Power Module in this book and the next chapter for additional ideas about playing with your baby as they grow.

Remember to continue your role as historian and cameraman during these early days at home. You will want to capture plenty of these play moments and other times. Your child will love to watch the video in their later years and you will enjoy seeing what your hair looked like back then. Keep the video camera handy and don't put it off until later. These days will fly by fast.

Break Time

It is crucial for your wife to get some playtime as well during the first weeks at home. And I don't mean playtime with the baby—she is likely getting plenty of that. You need to see to it that she has some playtime by herself and with you.

Think of it this way. Your wife has just started a new job that requires twenty-four hours a day, seven days a week. She is now a mom. Every human needs a break from his or her responsibility. You have to come up for air. Even during a regular workday you have to pause to eat lunch and take a break. The same need applies to a brand new mom.

The other key playtime you and your wife need is dating, just the two of you.

A new mom needs the opportunity to get out of the house *by herself* during the first few weeks at home. There is no true alone/play time at home because she is still on call even if the baby is sleeping, and she is also still on call when she takes the baby out with her. You can help by making sure that on a regular basis she has the opportunity to get out for an hour or two or three without being on call. Ideally you should supply the on duty baby care while she is out during the first few weeks. A trusted grandparent or very close friend may be another option. Help your wife get that time out by herself.

The other key playtime you and your wife need is dating, just the two of you. You both need to be off duty and together so you can talk and continue building your awesome relationship. In the early weeks, it can be hard for you both to leave the baby behind for a couple of hours while you go out. If you have that grandparent or friend who can help, then go for it. Try to schedule your time out when you expect the baby to be sleeping. Even thirty minutes out together for a cup of coffee gets you on the dating road again. If it doesn't look like just the two of you can go, then bring the baby out with you. Again, try to hit a time when Baby is likely to be sleeping so you and your wife can focus on each other. Be an encourager and leader in getting dates going. Everyone will benefit.

What About Me?

Last, but certainly not least, you need to have some time for yourself. While you need the playtime with your baby and wife just addressed, you also need some time by yourself to clear your head and take care of yourself.

The key to this alone playtime in these early weeks is *when* you take it. If you are working outside the home, you should consider your commute time or your lunchtime as part of that alone time to clear your head. The definition of playtime we are using here is off duty from baby responsibility. So if it helps, you could consider your entire workday playtime. How is that for a change of perspective?

You might consider bumping your schedule around some to get in the time needed. My favorite alone time slot is early in the morning between 5:00 a.m. and 6:00 a.m. when everyone else in the house is usually sleeping. It is a great time to exercise or read. It is also a great time to pay bills, prepare a world-class evening meal, or do other tasks. Consider turning the TV off at night and going to bed an hour earlier. Then get up an hour earlier to have some quality "you time" on the front end of your day.

To agitate you even further, I suggest that you take very little alone time for yourself on the weekends in the early weeks of having a newborn at home. If you are working a standard Monday through Friday type job, this is especially true. Your wife is likely counting on your extra help with Baby during the weekend and hoping to get some time out alone. So don't work all week and then inform her you'll be playing eighteen holes of golf on

Saturday and going to the game on Sunday. The first forty days at home and beyond is a time of personal sacrifice. You signed up for this and you need to see it through. You will have more you time down the road.

One idea for the weekends is trading on duty time with your wife. Work it out where she takes an hour or two out of the house and then later you get your hour or two out to exercise, read, run errands, or do your fun thing of choice. Having some scheduled times can take away the stress of not knowing when you are going to get out. The key is communication and being flexible in your play schedule.

So why all the fuss about the play *P*? Because having a baby can be a hard and stressful time. Playing helps you rejuvenate. It helps you to not take yourself too seriously as you learn new things. It keeps your marriage alive. It keeps you involved with your new baby. Above all it helps you stay fresh and ready to push on to the next day and the next adventure in parenting.

Beyond the Forty-Day Dash

The first forty days at home with a newborn are incredible. It is a busy time full of new things and adjustments. As you can see, there is plenty of work to do. The first year of your baby's life will hold more challenges. Amazingly, it just keeps getting better. And you will grow and get better as well. You really can become the super dad and husband you are intended to be. Enjoy!

FATHER, grant us new wisdom and energy as we go through these first weeks at home with our new baby. Double the power of each hour of sleep we get. Bless my wife with a smooth recovery and bless our baby with wonderful health. Let us all learn new skills. May others come around and provide support and encouragement when we need it. Lord, let this new life grow our marriage even stronger and bring us many new joys. In the name of our life's Architect we pray, **AMEN.**

Wisdom to Consider

"Love is patient, love is kind.
It does not envy, it does not boast,
it is not proud. It is not rude,
it is not self-seeking, it is not easily
angered, it keeps no record of wrongs.
Love does not delight in evil
but rejoices with the truth.
It always protects, always trusts,
always hopes, always perseveres."

I CORINTHIANS 13:4–7

Everyone in your new family needs lots of love. Lead the way.

☑ CHAPTER CHECKLIST

❑ Be present (physically and mentally) for your wife during these first forty days at home. When away from the house always be reachable by phone for consult and support.

❑ Go to your baby's first several checkup appointments and participate. Go with your wife to her six-week follow-up appointment and participate.

❑ Protect your new family's time and energy level by limiting commitments. Learn to say no to some things and support your wife in doing the same.

❑ Protect your wife's physical recovery. Help with the household chores and heavy lifting. Do whatever you can to make sure she gets rest.

❑ Listen (really listen) to your wife as she recovers from childbirth and takes on her new role as mother. Be watchful for the signs of postpartum depression. Support and encourage her *every* day.

❑ Be aware of your own emotions and moods. Be flexible and don't let little things get to you. Don't rush your wife into returning to your sex life too soon.

❑ Read again the "do and don't" Protector section of this chapter. Absorb and remember them.

❑ Don't be afraid to consult your pediatrician regarding the health of your baby. You aren't bothering them. Trust your instincts and your wife's instincts if you think something is wrong. Be especially vigilant for any fever in an infant.

- ❏ Review the checklists from earlier chapters to make sure you are caught up on all your to do's. Make sure your head, hands, and wallet are all in the game.

- ❏ Give lots of extra love to your wife during this time. Hugs, notes, kind words, and lots of helping actions are a great start.

- ❏ Provide leadership by pulling things onto your plate. Help steer offers for help from family and friends. Lead by example with healthy food, exercise, and lifestyle choices. Help your wife with these as well.

- ❏ Be the spiritual leader in your home. Pray with your wife. Pray for your baby, for each other, and for your marriage. Go to church.

- ❏ Work with your wife to get a list of household tasks for you to handle. Cooking, cleaning, laundry, shopping, and others are all fair game. Take on some new chores, stick with them, and get them done on time.

- ❏ Help take care of this baby! Diapering, bathing, dressing, feeding, burping, soothing, and more are on your list. Learn and do more than your share.

- ❏ Work closely with your wife on the baby's feeding routine, especially the nighttime program. Do all you can to help. Know your assignments before you both go to sleep.

- ❏ Be involved with the day-to-day decision making involving your baby. Work with your wife. Remember two heads are always better than one.

- ❏ Play with that new baby. Talking, reading, and showing them things are great starters. Unwrap them so they can move and kick. Take some pictures.

❑ Make sure your wife gets out of the house *by herself* for some free time while you watch the baby. Do this as often as possible so she can relax.

❑ Go on some dates with your wife during these first forty days. Ideally just the two of you should go, even if it is for a quick break, meal, or walk.

❑ Schedule some you-time to regroup as well. Try not to do this on the weekend unless you are trading out time squarely with your wife.

Chapter 8

The First Year

▶ Being a first time parent is the toughest job you and your wife will ever have. It is both physically and mentally challenging. That is why God designed children to come along at an age when you are at the top of your life's physical and mental health capacity.

The best news is that having children can also be the best times of your life. As mentioned before, the rewards are huge. The spiritual and marital growth you will get are everlasting. After a few months of living with a baby, you won't be able to imagine your life without that child. Being a father is an awesome job with awesome responsibilities and rewards.

As you head off into the rest of your first year of parenting, your to do list won't be getting any shorter. Babies grow fast and change a lot in the first year. You will have to move quickly to keep up with them. So saddle up and let's see what it takes to hang on.

Wagon Scout

In the early American pioneer days, wagon trains moved from the east to the new frontier in the west. While the wagons lumbered along, a scout rode ahead on his trusty horse to find the best route. He looked for danger, analyzed the weather, and scouted the terrain. He also assessed the overall condition of the people in his care and decided what they could handle. And then, after consulting with other leaders in the party, the group made decisions on which way to go and when. The scout's job was to make sure he got the group safely from point A to point B every day.

As a dad you have much of the scouting responsibility for your family. Working side by side with your wife, you will be getting your party through each day and through the first year. One trusty horse you will be riding especially hard this year is the Protect *P*. Your new baby and your wife both need your help here.

A big part of your job in the first year is to also give the baby a secure and protected environment to hang out in.

Let's take a look first at what Baby needs. We have already covered a number of important to do items, such as immunizing, sleeping babies on their backs, and watching for fever. A big part of your job in the first year is to also give the baby a secure and protected environment to hang out in.

One thing you need to remain vigilant on in this category is car seat safety. When traveling in a car your baby MUST remain in a properly installed, rear facing car seat. Your baby will be rear facing until he or she achieves BOTH minimum standards of one year old and twenty pounds in weight.[7] The seat must be the proper size for Baby's weight and it must be installed securely. Your job is to check the installation regularly—it needs to be tight with no side-to-side or up-and-down movement. If you often have to move your baby's seat or base from car to car, consider getting two setups. That way you can leave both tightly secured and you or your wife won't do an incorrect or loose installation when you get in a hurry. If you still don't feel like you have things installed correctly, go back to the directions or get help from another person in the know.

The other area you need to scout and secure for your baby's first year is your home. Because they are not mobile at all, this might seem unnecessary when you first bring your baby home. But babies develop extremely fast. Within the first year they will pull up, crawl, and even walk. You will be well served to start child proofing before then and get ahead of the curve. Once they are on the move it quickly changes everything.

No list of child proofing to do's can ever be all-inclusive as each home is so different. In your house you will see some things in need of change not discussed here. Remember, babies don't have any common sense and they are counting on you to lend them yours for a while. Look around your own home with the objective eye of a good wagon scout and get it ready. Here is a list to get you started:

- Get down on the floor at infant level and look around. You may find some interesting hazards and some corners to be cleaned.
- Cover all electrical outlets with plastic outlet covers. Hide and manage electrical cords as much as possible to prevent chewing and pulling. Out of sight is out of mind and out of mouth.
- Put breakables up and out of babies reach. You may want to have one off-limit item within babies reach for some no-no training. Babies need to start to learn they can't touch everything and this can be a way to ease them into it.
- Put safety gates at the top and bottom of all stairways.
- Secure all heavy furniture to the wall such as dressers and bookcases. Babies climb and with the right leverage can pull things over.
- Use doorknob covers for doors you want to keep closed for Baby. These will slow them down for a couple of years but still allow easy access for adults.

- Turn your hot water temperature down to 120 degrees or less. Degrees may be hard to measure. You should be able to hold your hands under pure hot water without pain. If you can't do this, turn down the temp.
- Install drawer and cabinet child locks or stops. You may want to leave one low cabinet open for the baby to have some plastic bowls, cups, and other safe items to play with. Some babies may figure your latches out, so be ready to change them or move more things up in the kitchen. In extreme cases you may decide to gate off the kitchen.
- Keep all kitchen knives and sharp utensils up high. No sharp knives or utensils should go in the dishwasher as Baby may learn how to open it.
- Keep all household cleaners, chemicals, and soaps up and out of reach or locked away. Do the same for your garage and keep that area locked and off limits if possible.
- Install covers or a guard on stove knobs to prevent baby access. Remember to cook on back burners as much as possible and keep pot handles turned to the back and away from tiny explorers.
- Move all plants up and off of the floor. Remove for now those cute plant stands that can be pulled over.
- Pad the sharp corners on all tables, furniture, and fireplaces. You can buy pad strips for this purpose. The pads might not look sexy but they can keep your infant out of the emergency room.
- Look at the handles and knobs on your furniture as well. Consider changing them out if they are sharp or could cause injury in a fall.
- Put window stickers on large glass doors or windows. Your fast crawling or walking baby might think that big chunk of glass is not there and hit it at full speed.

- Make sure your crib is assembled correctly and sturdy. Don't use antique cribs or even the one you or your wife had as a child. Look for a JPMA label to make sure your crib is up to current safety standards. Slats need to be no more than 2 3/8 inches apart.
- Look around your home for chipped paint on windows, baseboards, and elsewhere. Fix it. You may see it as a nuisance, but your baby sees it as something to snack on.
- Make sure the cords on window blinds and drapes are safe. These can be extremely dangerous for babies. Those manufactured prior to 2001 are not up to current safety standards. Visit the Window Covering Safety Council Web site at www.windowcoverings.org to learn more. They can also send you free kits and instructions to retrofit many models of older window coverings.
- Install toilet seat latches to keep your child out of what they see as miniature swimming pools. Remember a child can drown in as little as two inches of water.
- Keep all bathroom items such as soap, shampoo, deodorant, toothpaste, vitamins, medication, makeup, nail polish, and razors up and out of Baby's reach.
- Do the same for other household items such as plastic bags, matches, sewing supplies, office supplies, jewelry, beads, and older kid's toys with small pieces.
- Scout around for other items at baby level your child may want to eat. Look for things like candy, coins, and pet food.
- Look for trip points for your new unsteady walker. Loose rugs and carpet can be prime suspects. Fix them or get rid of them.
- Inspect all stair railings and banisters. Make sure nothing is loose or in need of repair. Slats should be less than

four inches apart. If they aren't, replace them or install a plastic barrier.

→ Consider replacing glass-top tables now, or install a heavy pad on them until your child is older. They are just asking to be broken with a toddler around.

→ Recheck your fire extinguishers, smoke alarms, carbon monoxide alarm, and first aid kit. If you still don't have these items, get them now and install them.

→ Make sure visitors' purses and jackets are kept up high and away from Baby. Your explorer could find medications, cosmetics, car keys, and cherished items that aren't for them.

Consider working through this list with grandparents or other homes your little cruiser might be visiting frequently. You might not be able to create the same environment as your own home, but at least you can create awareness and some safe areas. Most grandparents will appreciate the refresher course and knowing their home is baby safe as well.

Toy Story

A good scout will be taking a hard look at the toys and equipment Baby will use. Make sure jumpers, swings, and stationary play vehicles like "exersaucers" are put together correctly and used in a safe place. Toys like this can loosen up after use so give them a look periodically to make sure all fasteners are tight and in place.

You and your wife should also be screening the toys coming into your home. Even though a toy is designed and labeled for three-year-olds and up doesn't mean a well intended gift giver wouldn't present it to your six-month-old for Christmas. Pay particular attention to any toy or pieces that pose a choking hazard. A general rule of thumb is if a toy, piece of a toy, or other object can fit inside a toilet paper roll then it is too small for any child under three years old. If you get some gifts within this category, politely thank the giver and then put the toy on a high closet shelf as soon as possible. You will have a three-year-old before you know it and you will appreciate having a stockpile of toys available. Use the toilet paper roll test as you look around your house for other choking hazards.

Your task is to do the best job you possibly can baby proofing your home. You don't want to live in a fully padded, boring room with no water or electricity nor does your baby. They are hard wired to explore and you need to let them. Just be a good scout and help make sure their travels are as safe as possible.

Partner Protection Please

At some point in your parenting career someone may suggest you are being over protective of your child. Consider replying with something like, "Thank you, I am very protective of my family." If you aren't protecting your children, who is? Dude, this is *your job*. And the same level of protection you bring to your children in this crucial time must also extend to your wife.

As discussed earlier, childbirth and the months following can wreak havoc on many women. The female body produces all kinds of hormone surges, some high and some low, during this time. On top of this, your wife's mental and physical capacities are being stretched to the max with all of the new baby chores and decisions to make.

It is estimated that 50 percent to 75 percent of women have the baby blues at some point following delivery.[8] This can be characterized by sadness, moodiness, stress, anger, anxiety, loss of appetite, disinterest in the baby, or inability to function and make decisions. About 10 percent to 15 percent of mothers will experience the more severe symptoms of postpartum depression within the first year after giving birth.[9] This is characterized by longer and more severe bouts of the symptoms listed. Finally, nearly every new mother on the planet will experience some mental and physical fatigue during the first year. Babies are hard work and they make you tired!

So what is a guy to do? The answer is help. As real men we must help our wives and families through these storms when they come along. *The most important list of to do's in this book follows here.* These are things you should be doing anyway, regardless of your wife's physical and mental state. So don't wait for your wife to hit rock bottom before you decide to engage. Get on course with these right away:

- ↦ Watch for signs of the baby blues, postpartum depression, and fatigue. The signs can show up days or even months after delivery. Talk with your wife regularly about how she is feeling, and listen—really listen—to her feedback.

- ↦ Avoid burying your head in the sand of work. Once a baby arrives many men tend to get lost in their work as a way to provide. You can still provide and be an aware and involved father at home.

- ↦ Help take the sharp edges off the household and baby workload. Walk into your home each day like a newcomer and see the work that needs doing. Wives often lament, "Can't you see what I have to do?" See it and help get things done. Ask again how you can help if you really don't know.

- ↦ Let conflicts with your wife cool for a day. Chances are the majority won't be important in twenty-four hours. Those that still are can be addressed when you can have an adult conversation, preferably in the early or middle part of the day when you are both better rested.

- ↦ Encourage your wife and thank her for all she is doing. Many women constantly analyze their performance as a mother and ask the downer question, "Am I a bad mom?" Don't let her talk herself into a negative answer. Remind her of all the great things she is doing.

→ Remember your wife could be going from the social hero in her circle of friends to the social zero tied at home to a crying baby. Get her some time out of the house WITHOUT the baby.

→ Moms need the friendship and support of other moms. Help your wife connect with at least one other responsible mother in your neighborhood. They can support each other emotionally and help take care of each other's children for short breaks and errand running.

→ Remember, women want to raise their children and share the experience with someone they love. Don't be a casual observer—be an active participant. Let her know she is well loved and well supported.

→ Pray daily with your wife and ask for what you both need to get through the stressful times: energy, wisdom, patience, happiness, good health, and calm.

→ Help ensure your wife is getting the right amount of these wonder drugs: exercise, balanced diet, rest, sunshine, and outside oxygen.

→ Seek medical help and counseling if necessary. If your wife is struggling emotionally or shows signs of postpartum depression, don't keep it a secret from her physician. These are real medical conditions that can be treated very successfully.

Our six-year-old son helped bring all of this into perspective as I was putting him to bed one night. On the way out of the living room, I asked him to thank his mother for all she did for him that day. He looked back at us and asked in disbelief, "Did Mom do things for me today?" My wife smiled and patiently reminded him of the clothes she washed for him, the lunch she made for him, the teeth she brushed for him, the books she read to him, and about a dozen other items. (I think she also threw in birthing him for good measure.) You could see the wheels turning in his head. Up until then his six-year-old mind took all of these things for granted. They were automatic. They were no longer seen as needing praise or thanks or recognition. Don't let yourself become that six-year-old. Don't take for granted what your wife is contributing to your family every hour of every day. Thank her and help her.

As you can see, the wagon scout and his trusty Protection *P* horse have a lot of ground to cover in the first year. Your job as Dad is to make sure *all members of your family* get safely through this first year and beyond. Keep your scout eyes and ears sharp, and you will handle the trail and enjoy the ride.

More First Year Baby Stuff

After a few weeks with a new baby much of the outside world won't be knocking on your door to help out. Free meals, assistance, and congratulations will begin to dry up. Everyone assumes you have it figured out and all is well. So that leaves you and your wife to do all of the heavy lifting. And to be successful you have to be good partners.

Good partners team up on tasks and share the baby workload, just like sharing the household workload. The next section of this book is made up of twenty Power Modules. Each is a short summary of a baby or family task aimed at giving you the "power" to be a great partner. Topics include diapering, feeding, burping, dressing, bathing, and more. While these pages can help you get started, nothing will replace on-the-job training with your own baby. Learn the basics presented here and then expand your skills with your own little one. If you do you will be on your way to a great partnership.

Depending on your baby, one of the hardest commodities to come by in the first year can be sleep—or getting enough of it. I put this at the top of the partnering list. Until your baby is sleeping through the night you should be partnering with your wife on the nighttime routine. To put it simply, you should be at least as tired as your wife. Every baby is different and will start sleeping through the entire night at different times. These times won't last forever and you need to take the lead and help everyone "gut" through the tough times.

Have faith that a day (night) will come when your baby sleeps through without waking. It is a beautiful thing.

If you have a baby who is not sleeping through the night, you will find plenty of resources to help. Your pediatrician, friend's advice, and books on the topic can all help you and your wife frame your own plan of attack. If part of your plan involves letting the baby cry it out at an appropriate age, you need to be especially supportive of your wife. No mother can stand to let a baby cry for very long, so you need to step up and take the front line duty if this is part of your strategy. Have faith that a day (night) will come when your baby sleeps through without waking. It is a beautiful thing.

The American Academy of Pediatric Dentists recommends your child have their first dental exam by age one.[10] Just because they only have a few teeth doesn't mean you shouldn't go. Your dentist will be teaching you how to properly brush your infant's teeth and how to reduce the discomfort of erupting new teeth. One of the best things you can do as a parent is to release your grown child into the world with a beautiful smile, and that responsibility starts in year one.

Another thing you might hear a lot about, especially from friends with babies, is percentile rankings. Your physician will be recording height, weight, and head circumference at checkups.

The main purpose for this is to track the growth of your child and to make sure they are progressing properly. Remember that, like many other things in life, bigger isn't always better, so don't fall into the trap of "percentile envy."

You will undoubtedly have friends who tell you their child is "so big for their age" and "off the charts." Good for them. If your little bundle of joy is at the fifth or fiftieth or ninety-fifth percentile, he or she is fine. Size at this age is not totally indicative of adult size or success in life. This is just good practice for when the same friends tell you how their three-year-old is a piano virtuoso and a starter on the varsity basketball team at preschool. Good for them. Just smile and know your baby is *really* the smartest and most beautiful in the world.

You will want to be on the same page as your partner concerning many other items. Here are a few to talk through and agree on:

- → *Daily and nightly schedule:* Babies thrive with a good routine. Agree on what the routine is and who has what duties and when.
- → *Babysitters and daycares:* You should both be involved in the selection process. Two brains and hearts are better than one when making these important selections.
- → *Early discipline and structure:* Agree on what things constitute a no from both parents. This is the root of consistency you will need as your child grows older.

Dollars and Sense

Throughout the first year you will want to continue analyzing your financial situation. Is your wife now thinking about NOT returning to work? Have you reworked your budget to allow for diapers, baby food, and other baby items? Did you get that big life insurance policy yet? These questions and others need answers. Go back to the chapter on Getting Your Wallet in the Game and make sure you are up to full speed.

A big topic couples wrestle with in this category is with Mom returning to work. The choice for you and your wife may be easy. But lots of couples out there are on the fence. You both may find yourself changing your minds over time. If you are on the fence, sit down together and work through the emotions. Then go through the financials and see if you can come up with a work-able plan.

Whether you are working, disabled, or deceased, your baby is counting on you to provide.

Another area couples need to watch is insurance. Go back and review the insur-ance material presented earlier and make sure your health, life, dis-ability, and other coverages are where they need to be. Remember, whether you are working, disabled, or deceased, your baby is count-ing on you to provide. This is your obligation, so get covered.

Money is the number-one issue couples have disagreements over. Your money situation will be tighter when your baby arrives so be careful not to let disagreements accelerate out of control. Money disagreements can be fueled by lack of communication, different backgrounds and understandings, different expectations, and different spending habits.

To keep a lid on these money fires, you and your wife need to commit to each other. Have regular planned discussions at least every other week, if not every week, about how and where things are going. Have realistic expectations, goals, and spending habits. Build a budget and spend each dollar on paper before it arrives in your bank account. Be good shoppers and use competition to your advantage. Remember, together you can win!

The Love Boat

As the first year with Baby rolls on, many marriage engines can start to sputter. The stress and strain and lack of sleep can take their toll. Don't let it happen. And if it does happen, work hard to get your marriage running smoothly again.

The key to your family's success (and we aren't defining success as money) is that strong marriage engine. If that puppy is sick or not hitting on all cylinders, everything around it runs poorly as well. For example, young children thrive in a home free of tension as much as adults. Here are some reminders to help keep your marriage engine running strong:

- → Take pride in your personal appearance. Don't let yourself go during these crazy times. Exercise, eat right, and dress nicely. And do it all for your wife as much as yourself. You are *one*.
- → Support your wife's efforts to do the same. Help her find time to exercise. Compliment her appearance and her work. Tell her how beautiful she is and how lucky you are to be going through life with her.
- → Date, date, date. This should be a top priority. Couples must have time away from the responsibility of a baby. Schedule it and make it a priority. And get fun with it—open her door, hold hands, steal a kiss, laugh, and be crazy in love. Share your heart.
- → Remember you can have romance without sex. Your wife will love you even more if you understand this.
- → Sometime in the first year people will ask when you are going to have *another* baby. Take your time, and don't let anyone or anything pressure you or your wife.

Leading in the Jungle

As you work hand in hand with your wife during this busy chapter of life, remember this analogy of management and leadership. Think of a work crew (your family) blazing a new trail through a thick jungle. The managers (you and your wife) are in charge of scheduling the workers, feeding them, making sure the machetes are sharpened, and keeping the group safe and motivated, among all the other tasks. But the leader is the one who has the courage to climb the tree, look over the land, and shout "wrong jungle" when necessary. Jungles include your priorities in life: the kind of family you want to be, your career, where you live, your chosen pursuits, your spiritual life, and more.

A leader helps get his team in the right jungles *and* helps manage the show on the ground. Make sure your family is in the right jungles and expending its time and energy on the right long-term things. And make sure you are helping out on the ground as well with diapers, bottles, baths, and cooking dinner. Climbing those trees and providing the love and leadership your family needs is a big deal. But it is what you were built for. The rewards are huge and the habits you set now will serve you well in future years.

Baby Playtime

As your child grows during the first year you will see amazing changes. Their capabilities will literally change from week to week. After three babies of my own and extensive research on the best toys and visual exercises to do with your child in this first year, I have narrowed it all down to one thing you can give your baby: time. That's it!

The precious commodity of your time is what your baby *really* wants and needs. Being in the same room working on your laptop while your baby toddles around is not enough. Meet them on their turf. Get down on the floor with them. Let them hear your voice and your encouragement. Be curious with them. This is the point in life where you really do get to be a kid again, so have some fun. Don't worry about pushing the education envelope as that will come soon enough. Let your baby be a baby. Relax and have a good time.

> This is the point in life where you really do get to be a kid again, so have some fun.

Like a lot of things in life you may need to schedule some time with your baby. But you will be at the mercy of their schedule, not yours. So don't think you can slot them in at 10:00 a.m. every Saturday for some quality one-on-one time. Instead, have some floating time slots on your agenda and when you see a good playtime opportunity, take it. And don't expect too many hour-long play marathons. Your baby's play energy and focus will increase over time. So be happy with a few minutes here and there if that is all they allow. You will know when the gig is up and they are ready to do something else.

During your playtime you still need to keep your protector hat on. This is especially true during those expeditions outside the house. Keep your baby comfortable, cool or warm, depending on the season. Remember to take things such as sunscreen and water. Watch out for bug bites and bee stings with new babies. Should they get a bite or sting, check them closely for any allergic reactions.

Watch over your baby in playgroups with other children as well. If the mosquito bite was a bad experience, wait until the neighbor's one-year-old tries to bite a chunk out of your baby's arm. You will need to gently referee some of the pushing and pulling as young minds wrestle with the concepts of sharing and playing together.

The best immune system possible is one of the most important things you can equip your child with if he or she is playing with others at this age. The three "R" wonder drugs for this are rest, routine, and right foods. That way your baby's system will be ready when the other child who was "just a little sick yesterday" hands them a nice saliva-coated toy.

Relish your role throughout this first year as historian. Work with your wife to build a memory book. Or if time doesn't allow for creating a masterpiece now, at least save the ingredients in a box so you can build one later. While pictures and video are the classic building blocks, consider some other memory makers as well. For example, my wife and I have written letters or brief notes to our children at different points in their first year sharing some special memories. Put these in your memory box. Save a special toy, blanket, clothing item, or other special keepsake during the first year as well. Someday your thirty-year-old baby will be so glad you took the time to preserve these treasures.

Present

We have saved the number-one *P* for last. Being present in the first year of your baby's life and the years beyond is huge. Be there or be square as they used to say. Or be cool and love the drool as they say now. Either way a baby is counting on a committed mother and father to carry them through the early years of life.

As a present father, one of the best things you do as you sharpen your parenting style is manage your own emotions. Many men are paralyzed by fears in fathering. It could be the fear of providing adequately, especially when you see the dollars flying out the door for food and diapers and clothes and college. Combat this fear with logical antibiotics: a sound budget, discussions with your wife, and an occasional side job if necessary. Don't let it consume you.

Another common fear is that of ability. Maybe your own father or lack of one is clouding your mind. Don't let it. Deal with the past appropriately and then write your own story. History does not have to repeat itself.

This leads to another emotion you need to get a hold of: anger. Men are full of the hormone testosterone. This is like our survival gasoline, but we need to manage the sparks in life that can cause us to blow. Mellow out, dude. Don't let the little stuff bug you like it used to. Get in the habit of knowing your kids are watching you and your reactions to things. Are you modeling how you want them to be? How you want them to treat their spouse? And don't be bitter about the lack of "me time." Know you will have plenty of time to yourself down the road. The chapter of life you are in now requires you to be unselfish. It requires the most you have in flexibility and understanding.

> *The chapter of life you are in now requires you to be unselfish. It requires the most you have in flexibility and understanding.*

One of the best things you can do as a new father is to find a mentor—a senior wagon scout from whom to learn. This is usually someone just a few years ahead of your family in the kid cycle. Find someone you respect with a healthy marriage and ask if you can learn from them. Have lunch together, and share your heart and your concerns. Listen to what that person has to say.

Remember that a man needs the company and community of other healthy men. There are a huge number of grown men without at least one true friend. Don't let yourself become isolated during these busy times. Life's lions love to cut you from the safety of the herd and pull you down. Men who become isolated can talk themselves into some pretty crazy things and get in some bad situations. A great man surrounds himself with wise counsel and some real friends. Doing this will do your soul and your family good.

Lastly, I suggest you keep learning. A number of other great books and resources are out there to draw from. A couple I recommend are the "Father" series of books from Armin Brott as well as the Heidi Murkoff's "What to Expect" series your wife may be reading. These resources in particular offer some great information and details for you to absorb. Keep your mind open to learning and you will be unstoppable.

Final Words

The foundation of this book is what you can do as a man to be a great husband and father. But even bigger than what *you do* is who *you are*. What is your character made of? Do you have real integrity? What are your core values and beliefs? Is your heart in the right place? Your answers are the building blocks you will lay all of your doing and checklist items upon.

A good self-evaluation is to ask whether you are a life-giving spirit to your family or a life-draining spirit on your family. Are your wife and kids excited when you come home at the end of the day? Or are they dreading when you walk through the door? Think about which man you want to be.

The world has many definitions of what a real man and father should be, but the best one I've seen is made of four key components and comes from a curriculum called Men's Fraternity.[11] It is combined here with key components from this book:

- → *A real man is one who rejects passivity.* Be present physically and mentally. Don't wait for that perfect time to get involved with the baby or household chores. Don't wait to bring up the tough budget discussions or to ask your wife how she is feeling. Do it now.
- → *A real man is one who accepts responsibility.* Provide and protect. You have a lot on your plate to do. Your family

is counting on you. Don't make excuses. Don't quit trying. Take responsibility for getting your wagon train safely
from point A to point B each and every day.

→ *A real man is one who leads courageously.* Lead by example.
Be a true partner. Give direction. Give love. Initiate play.
Climb the trees and make sure your family is in the right
jungles.

→ *A real man is one who expects God's greater reward.* Be led
and grounded by your faith, not your emotions. Know that
being a great father and husband are at the top of your to
do list every day.

Live this definition and you are well on your way to a life
focused on real significance rather than one focused on financial
and material success. Your wife will thank you, and some day your
children will too. Go get 'em, Dad.

FATHER, grant our baby safety in our home and in the outside world. Surround this child with safe and caring adults throughout life. Lord, see that my wife has special protection during these busy and stressful times. Guard our minds and our bodies. Let me understand the roles I can play and tasks I can take on to lead our home. Guide me to be the great man, husband and father You desire me to be. Allow our marriage to grow and run stronger than ever before. Thank You, God, for the gift of children and family and the responsibility that goes with them. In the name of the Creator of family we pray, **AMEN.**

Wisdom to Consider

"A baby will make love stronger,
days shorter, nights longer,
bankroll smaller, home happier,
clothes shabbier, the past forgotten,
and the future worth living for."

ANONYMOUS

A baby adds new life to your life. Do the best job you can and enjoy.

☑ CHAPTER CHECKLIST

❑ Recheck your child's car seat regularly and make sure it is tight and properly installed. Remember, your baby will be riding in a properly sized, rear facing car seat until he or she is at least one year of age and weighs twenty pounds.

❑ Baby proof your home before your infant begins crawling. Work through the home room-by-room using the checklist of items provided in this chapter. Help grandparents prep their home if your little one will be a frequent visitor.

❑ Recheck play equipment your baby is using like swings and "exersaucers" for loose parts and proper installation.

❑ Carefully evaluate all toys coming into the home. Screen small parts that present a choking hazard. Put up toys not age appropriate for later use. Keep an eye and ear out for toy manufacturer recalls.

❑ Watch diligently for signs of the baby blues or postpartum depression in your wife. Read again the items you can do to help that are presented in this chapter. Work to be a part of the solution and not part of the problem.

❑ Be a great partner and help with household chores and baby care chores. Work through the Power Module tasks presented in this book and become an expert at diaper changing, bathing, feeding, burping, dressing, calming, and the others.

❑ Do everything possible to help your wife get enough sleep, even if it means giving up some of your own. Work together to get your baby on a path to sleeping through the night.

- ☐ Go to all the well checkup appointments your baby has in the first year. Ask questions and listen to what your pediatrician has to say. Make sure your baby visits a dentist during the first year and learn how to take care of those new teeth.

- ☐ Continue to evaluate the possibility of one parent not working outside the home and staying with your child. If you can pull it off financially, you will be glad you did. If it isn't possible right now, and it is something you want to do, then get a plan and work toward the goal.

- ☐ Take another hard look at your insurance coverage. Make sure you have what you need. Check health, life, disability, homeowners or renters insurance, auto, and any other special coverage you might need.

- ☐ Work hard on keeping your marriage engine running strong. Don't neglect it. Work through the to do items presented in the chapter. Think regularly about what you can do to improve and make your marriage stronger. Make dating your wife a priority.

- ☐ Spend time with your baby! Play with them or even do nothing. Just be there.

- ☐ Start a keepsake box for your baby. Write some notes or letters to your little one to capture special moments in time and your thoughts. Collect some special photos and other items to put in there.

- ☐ Manage your own emotions. Overcome your fears and control your anger. No time is better than now to finish growing up.

- ☐ Seek out a mentor a few years ahead of you on the trail and learn from him. Find some other healthy men for friends. Don't let yourself become isolated.

❑ Keep learning! There are many excellent books, classes, and resources you can take advantage of. In addition to fathering skills, think about related topics like finances, job skills, leadership, relationships, marriage, and more.

❑ Keep the 5 P's as guideposts throughout life: be present, protect, provide, partner, and play. Be a real man, and be awesome!

How-To
Power
Modules

How to Clean a House—Fast!

Cleaning your home probably isn't on your list of favorite things to do. But with a plan and some determination, you can knock it out fast. The best first step is to schedule a time with yourself to do it. Consider naptime or before everyone wakes up in the morning (no vacuuming). Put on an old T-shirt and your iPod, move fast, and get it done.

How To

→ *Kill clutter.* To clean well, all horizontal surfaces must be visible. So first take care of the dirty dishes, toys, papers, and clutter. Make the beds and move the laundry.

→ *Simplify supplies.* You only need glass/multisurface cleaner, tub and tile cleaner, cleaning cloths, old toothbrush, scrubby sponge, duster, and trash bags. Carry all in a bucket or caddy from room to room. You will also need a mop and bucket.

→ *Attack the kitchen.* Spray sinks with cleaner and let it sit for a minute. Spray and wipe down counters, cabinets, and appliances. Finish the sink and take out the trash. Sweep the floor then mop.

→ *Police the bathroom.* Spray tub, shower, sink, and toilet with cleaners and let them to sit. Wipe mirrors clean and then counters. Go back to your tub and shower; scrub and then rinse clean. Do the same to sinks. Wipe faucets dry and shine. Move to the toilet and scrub with a brush or disposable cleaner. Spray the whole unit with Lysol disinfectant and wipe dry. Take out the trash, change the towels, and mop the floor.

→ *Do bedrooms and living areas.* Do a quick round of dusting. Finish killing any clutter, and fluff pillows. Clean the floors or vacuum. In the nursery remove any dirty diapers; wipe diaper-changing area with a damp cloth and dry.

Apply Other Tips:

→ Knock out one room at a time before moving on.

→ Pick a starting point and work your way clockwise around the room.

→ Lose the bar soap in bathrooms and replace with a liquid pump.

→ Wipe up and down or side to side; circles are wasted motion.

→ Begin mopping or vacuuming at the far end of the room and work your way to the door.

→ Warn your wife about wet floors so she doesn't slip and to earn some major cleaning points!

NOTES

How to Change a Diaper

You and your baby will do several *thousand* diaper changes together. Make it a fun time by talking or singing to your little one. Before you begin get all the gear you need within arms reach: fresh diaper, wipes, diaper rash cream, hand sanitizer (for you), and clean baby clothes if necessary.

How To

→ Place Baby face up on a clean, flat surface. If using a changing table, strap your baby in for safety. Always keep one hand on the baby. If right handed, put Baby's head to your left.

→ Remove what clothes are necessary to get to the action. Always remove Baby's socks prior to opening diaper.

→ Unfasten diaper and pull front down. This first blast of fresh air can cause Baby to pee some more, so after a second or two lay the front of the diaper back over the genitals to catch it.

→ Grab both of Baby's ankles with your left hand and lift slightly. If you are changing a poopy diaper, use the old diaper to make one front-to-back wipe to collect the majority of the blowout. Set dirty diaper to the side well out of Baby's reach.

→ Use wipes to gently clean Baby's bottom and genitals. In the first few weeks you may want to use warm washcloths instead, as they are gentler on brand-new skin. Be sure to wipe out leg creases and other folds in the area. Always wipe front to back on girls.

→ Apply diaper rash ointment only if necessary. Baby powder is not needed and can actually be a health hazard.

→ Lift ankles and use your right hand to slide a clean diaper under Baby's bottom. If using disposables, tabs will be at the back.

- →ı Bring diaper front up between legs to the stomach. On boys make sure penis is pointing down. Unpeel diaper tabs and fasten them to the front. The diaper should fit snug but not too tight. Check the back to make sure it is smooth and not creased.
- →ı Give your hands a shot of sanitizer, dress Baby, and move them on to the next party. Remember to circle back and clean up and properly dispose of the used diaper.

NOTES

How to Hold a Baby

People love to hold babies. That works out well as most babies love to be held. Good baby holding and carrying technique has two main purposes: to make the baby feel safe and secure and to make you feel safe and secure. Be sure in the early months to support Baby's head and neck until he or she can do it. You will eventually find the techniques and positions both you and Baby like for the mood and task at hand.

How To

→ *Front-face football carry.* Face Baby out with their back in the middle of your chest. Use one hand to support Baby's bottom and place the other hand across Baby's chest.

→ *Cradle hold.* Put Baby in the crook of either arm and hold snug against your chest. Baby should be slightly inclined. Wrap your other arm around to give support where needed. A great hold for bottle-feeding.

→ *Shoulder carry.* Face Baby toward you and gently hold against your chest and shoulder. Baby's chin should sit lightly on top of shoulder. Use hand from same side to support Baby's bottom. Use your other hand to hold against Baby's back and to support head and neck.

→ *Hip carry.* Use this hold only when Baby has good head and neck control. Face Baby in toward you and sit on your hipbone. Hold Baby snugly against you with your same side arm. Use your other arm to get some chores done.

→ *Astronaut hold.* Sit with your knees propped up. Lay Baby face up with head resting on your knees and thighs and with his or her feet on your stomach. Use your hands to steady. A great position for bottle feeding and talking to Baby.

→ *Belly hold.* Lay Baby face down straddling your forearm. The side of Baby's head should fit in your hand. Place your free arm on Baby's back to hold snug. Can also be done sitting with your forearm resting in your lap. Another variation is turning Baby so the head rests in your elbow joint.

→ *Slings, packs, and carriers.* These allow you to carry Baby in front of you or on your back, leaving your hands free. Always follow directions closely and make sure Baby is secure with head and neck supported if necessary.

_____

_____

_____

_____

_____

_____

_____

_____

_____

_____

_____

NOTES

How to Bottle Feed a Baby

Bottle-feeding is a great time for Dad to bond with Baby. Let your little one know you are present and that he or she is the most precious gift in the world.

Bottles should be properly sterilized and clean. If feeding formula you may find it easiest to make up a twenty-four-hour supply of bottles and refrigerate. Use boiled or super-filtered water when mixing formula. Use a nipple with the proper flow (slow, medium, fast) for your baby's age. With a newborn never leave home without a bottle, even for only a quick trip. Babies are not understanding of flat tires or running an extra errand. When it's time to eat, it's time to eat.

Never feed milk that is below room temperature. The preferred method of warming bottles is in hot water rather than a microwave because microwaves heat unevenly. If you choose to microwave, remove the lid and don't heat too much. Shake well after heating to eliminate hot spots. Check temperature on the inside of your wrist.

How To

→ Change diaper if necessary prior to feeding. Eating can make Baby drowsy, and a diaper change after feeding may wake them up.
→ Clear nipple prior to feeding. Turn bottle upside down and squeeze the nipple until milk comes out. Have milk land on your wrist to recheck temperature.
→ Outfit Baby with a bib or place a burp cloth under the chin.
→ Cradle Baby in your arm and against your side in a slightly upright position that supports the head. Hold the bottle with your other hand.

- Don't lay Baby flat for feeding or prop a bottle. Both are dangerous.
- Keep bottle at an angle where the nipple is always full during feeding. This helps prevent the baby from swallowing air.
- Burp as needed during feeding. A good rule of thumb is to do at least three burp sessions per feeding.
- Tickle Baby's chin if they are falling asleep before finishing a normal quantity. Don't force feed more if Baby seems uninterested.
- Dump unused milk from the bottle because it spoils quickly.

NOTES

How to Burp a Baby

Burping gets rid of air babies swallow during feeding. If babies aren't burped frequently, the swallowed air can lead to spitting up, gassiness, and discomfort. That is no fun for Baby or for you. As babies progress through the first year, they may burp less because they learn to swallow less air during feeding.

How To

→| Pat or rub Baby's back gently during burping. No pounding or hammering is necessary.

→| Keep a burp cloth handy to wipe away any spit-up or mess.

→| Do at least three burping sessions per feeding or every two to three ounces. Make sure one of those sessions is at the end of the feeding.

→| Try a different position if you don't get a burp after a couple of minutes. Try for a burp in the new position for a couple more minutes before going back to feeding.

→| Experiment with burping positions to find what works best for you and your baby. Try different variations of patting and rubbing high and low on Baby's back to find the sweet spot.

→| Keep Baby slightly upright for ten to fifteen minutes after feeding to help keep the milk down.

→| Classic shoulder position: Put a burp cloth over your right shoulder. Sit and hold Baby against your chest/shoulder area. Baby's stomach should be right against your collarbone and the chin should rest on your shoulder. Support Baby's bottom with your right hand. Hold Baby's head gently against your shoulder with your cheek. Use your left hand to gently pat Baby's back. Gentle movement in a rocking chair in this position may also help.

→ Lap sit position: Hold Baby sitting up in your lap. Place a burp cloth between your hand and Baby's chest, then flip the cloth over the back of your hand. Support Baby's chest and head with one hand. The heel of your hand should be on Baby's chest, and the chin should sit in the *U* of your thumb and index finger. Lean Baby forward and use your free hand to gently pat or rub the back.

NOTES

How to Swaddle a Baby

Swaddling is the age-old practice of wrapping a newborn snugly in a blanket. This helps the baby feel warm and secure, just like in the womb. It also helps limit sudden arm movements that can startle and wake a baby. You will want to experiment with blankets to see which work best for your swaddling. You and your baby will probably land on a favorite or two.

Some babies like swaddling and some don't. Take cues from your little one and decide if he or she enjoys it or not. A looser wrap with arms out might be an alternative. Don't swaddle a baby in an overly warm room as overheating is a risk factor for SIDS (sudden infant death syndrome). Most babies should not be swaddled after two months of age because it limits movement and can become a safety hazard as your baby learns to roll over. Check with your pediatrician on specific swaddling guidelines.

How To

→ Lay a blanket out in front of you in the shape of a diamond.
→ Fold the top tip of the blanket down about the width of the palm of your hand.
→ Lay your baby near the top of the blanket with the folded edge line in the middle of the back of the neck.
→ Bring Baby's right arm down to their side. Take the corner of the blanket to their right and pull it across the body. Tuck it underneath their left side.
→ Bring the bottom corner of the blanket up and tuck it inside the blanket near Baby's chest.
→ Bring Baby's left arm down to the side. Take the corner of the blanket to their left and pull it across the body. Tuck it beneath their right side.
→ Wa-la! One happy baby burrito.

How to Give a Baby a Bath

Bath time can be great fun for you and your baby. Until your little one is crawling and getting messier, a bath every two or three days with some wipe downs on the off days is adequate. Still, some parents choose to bathe their baby every day.

It is a good idea to avoid a tub bath during the first couple of weeks. This allows the umbilical cord stump to fall off and for circumcisions on boys to heal. During this time you can give a sponge bath, which is a good top-to-bottom wipe down with a warm, wet washcloth.

How To

→ Bring your gear to the bath site: baby tub, hooded towel, baby soap and shampoo, clean diaper, and clothes. The kitchen is a good area to use because most baby tubs fit in the sink, the lighting is good, and a few splashes of water won't hurt anything.

→ Put two or three inches of warm water in the tub. Undress your baby.

→ Carefully lower your baby into the tub, being careful to support the head. Talk and reassure. Keep Baby warm by pouring water on them throughout the bath. Never leave your baby unattended in the tub even for a second!

→ Wash from top to bottom with a slightly soapy washcloth—front first then back. Get in all the hiding places and in between those little fingers and toes. Rinse with a clean washcloth and warm water. Wash scalp last with a few drops of baby shampoo and rinse with water from your washcloth.

→ If your baby is having a good time, let them relax for a couple of minutes and enjoy the water. If they are upset, the party is over.

→ Get a good grip and remove your baby from the tub. Wrap them in a hooded towel, pat dry, diaper, and dress.

How to Dress a Baby

With spit-up, blowouts, bath time, and other adventures, your baby will likely need several costume changes each day. Dressing a floppy and sometimes unhappy tiny human in tiny clothes can be a challenge. But with a little practice, you will become a pro.

Remember to have fun. Dressing is a great time to talk and bond with your baby. Be super gentle and patient as you go. When choosing clothes, think comfort and cotton whenever possible. Babies can get cold fast without clothes on, so make sure your clothes are handy and you get with it. Dress Baby in layers as appropriate. Use a blanket for an extra layer when going outside because it is easier to put on and off Baby than a coat.

How To

→ Gather all of your gear, including a freshly diapered baby, onesie or T-shirt, and clothes or pajamas.

→ Stretch neck, arm, and leg holes out because the laundry will have tightened them up.

→ Choose a good dressing location, such as diaper changing table, bed, or soft floor. Lay Baby flat.

→ Bunch material at the neck for top layers. This will allow you to pull the clothing item over the baby's face in one quick peek-a-boo move.

→ Start at the crown of the head and ease the clothing item over the baby's face and then over the back of the head. Give good support to the head.

→ Bunch sleeve material up, reach through the bottom with your fingers and find Baby's hand. Gently pull hands and arm through. It is much easier to work it from that side than trying to shove baby arms through from the top.

- Be careful of tiny fingers and thumbs so they don't get bent the wrong way when making the trip through sleeves.
- Snap or button the upper body layer.
- Do the same bunch-find-pull with pants as you did with arms. Snap and button. Install socks, booties, or soft shoes if necessary.
- Repeat process with other layers as necessary.
- Be extra careful with zippers. Pull away from Baby's skin when closing to avoid any pinch.
- Congratulate yourself and Baby on a job well done and move on to your next adventure!

NOTES

How to Calm a Crying Baby

Babies rely on crying as the main way to communicate their desires. All babies cry and some cry more than others. Don't let long crying spells shake your confidence or make you feel inadequate. Partner with your spouse and work through the tough spells together as a team. Consult with your pediatrician if you need to and make sure you are doing everything possible.

The key to calming a crying baby is working through a logical order of trouble-shooting. Think of diagnosing a troubled engine and rule out one category before going to the next. Go at your crying engine (baby) in this order: fuel (food), air (burp), spark (sleep), and compression (comfort).

How To

→ı See if Baby is hungry. Have them nurse or give them a bottle.
→ı Try to burp Baby.
→ı Provide Baby a pacifier (it's like a comforting desert).
→ı Make sure Baby has a clean diaper.
→ı Try to move Baby into sleep:
  - swaddle
  - rock or hold
  - lay down (some babies like to get there on their own).
→ı If the above fuel/air/spark remedies aren't working, then work on comfort:
  - Make sure your baby is healthy. Does he or she have a fever, for example? If you suspect anything is wrong, contact your doctor.
  - Make sure clothing and diaper aren't pinching, rubbing, or aggravating Baby in any way.
  - Make sure Baby is not in an overly stimulating room with noise, people, and lights. Go to a quiet room with low lights.

- While holding try the magic shh-shh-shh sound constantly in Baby's ear. It simulates what was heard for so long in the uterus.
- Try holding Baby differently, or try holding less.
- Try movement with rocking, baby swing, bouncy seat, or carrying in a front pack or sling.
- Distract Baby with a toy, song, story, or look in the mirror.
- If your baby is teething, try remedies in that area.
- Try noise. Some babies are soothed by running water, white noise (radio static), clothes dryer hum, or music.
- Take Baby for a walk outside or a drive.
- Give Baby a warm bath if they like baths.
- Switch pitchers if necessary. Do all you can before calling in your wife. If she can't do the trick, then work out shifts where you each handle cry duty while the other rests and regains composure.

NOTES

How to Wrestle a Car Seat— and Win!

The proper mating of a child's car seat and the seat of your car is not as easy as it might seem. Research from the National Highway Traffic Safety Administration (NHTSA) shows that 70 percent or more of all car seats may be improperly installed or used. Your job is to be in the 30 percent doing it right.

Several great resources are on the Web for information on installation, use, safety, and selection. Among the best is the NHTSA site at www.NHTSA.gov. Here you can enter your zip code to locate a certified inspection station that can check your installation for free. It also has ease-of-use ratings for seats to help you in your purchase decisions.

Other good car seat information sites to check out:

→ www.AAP.org (American Academy of Pediatrics)
→ www.carseatsite.com
→ www.car-safety.org
→ www.consumerreports.org (lots of consumer product information)
→ www.safekids.org (also has lots of other good child safety info)

How To

→ Read BOTH car seat manual and car manual for proper installation.
→ Remember infants must ride rear facing until at least twenty pounds and one year of age. The safest place is the middle of the rear seat of your car. Never install in the front seat because of air bags' proximity.

- Don't use older or questionable seats you don't know the history on.
- Know how to do both a LATCH install and a seat-belt install.
- With a five-point harness, make sure it is in slots at or below Baby's shoulders.
- Ensure Baby is snug in the harness. Avoid heavy clothes or coats. Use a blanket to cover Baby if you need another layer.
- Place seat at correct angle so Baby's head doesn't flop forward. Use a folded towel under the seat to adjust the angle if necessary.
- Use ALL your weight to push the seat into your car seat when installing and taking up the slack. Lay on it or use your knee.
- Check your installation regularly. The seat should be tight with no more than an inch of movement in any direction.
- Take Baby in and out of car curbside and never street side.

NOTES

How to Pray for Your Baby

As a parent you need to pray consistently for your baby. After all, if you aren't praying for them, who is? Raising a healthy and happy baby is a huge task, and in today's world you need all of the help you can get!

The key to praying for children is not falling into the same rut of words we sometimes use at the dinner table (bless this food). Think hard about what your child needs and what you want them to be. Break it down into two categories: the immediate (sleeping through the night) and the long term (a loving healthy family of their own). Take one or two topics from the immediate and long term, and expand your prayer for that day around those. Keep it fresh and leave no stone unturned.

How To

→ Pray at least nightly over your child while they sleep or in another room if you fear waking them.
→ Pray together out loud with your wife. If you are still working toward this, pray on your own until you both get there.
→ While you have God on the phone, pray for your marriage and your parenting skills. Pray for wisdom, energy, love, and growth.
→ Immediate need examples: Pray that your child will have ...
  • Sleep through the night and good naps when needed
  • Relief from teething pain
  • Healthy checkups and easy immunizations
  • Safety at home and outside the home
  • Good eating habits that agree with the stomach.
→ Long term need examples: Pray your child will have ...
  • Salvation and belief in God

- A love of God's Word and a desire to read and understand it
- Good decision-making
- A strong, healthy body and mind
- Respect for their body and the bodies of others
- Good friends, teachers, coaches, and adult influences
- Honesty, respect, and a belief in hard work
- Respect for God's laws, the laws of the land, and authority
- Protection from the world's addictions such as drugs, alcohol, gambling, and overindulgence
- Courage, kindness, generosity, contentment
- Proper self-esteem and confidence
- A wonderful spouse, a strong marriage, and healthy, happy children of their own.

NOTES

How to Play with a Baby

Your child's physical, intellectual, and social development begins with play. And your baby loves when you play with and teach him or her things. You are your baby's first and most important teacher. And this is your chance to be a goofy kid again—so get down there and have some fun!

Time (yours) is king with Baby when it comes to play. You don't need a lot of high-tech toys or equipment, just some distraction-free time to devote to your little one. On the flip side, your baby doesn't need constant entertainment from you either. He or she will enjoy hanging out in the same room with you while they learn and practice things on their own.

How To

0–3 months

→ Talk and sing to Baby; hold them and walk around.
→ Shake a rattle or other toy near Baby. Slowly move it and see if they will follow it with their eyes.
→ Pour water from a cup on Baby in the bathtub. Squeak a duck and see if they can follow it.
→ Let Baby watch toys on a mobile. Talk to them about each one.

3–6 months

→ Read books and play music. Great at all ages, but you begin to get more interest around this age.
→ Lay with Baby on a blanket outside and talk about the things you see, such as trees, clouds, birds, grass, cars, and people.

- → Place Baby on a play mat with toys suspended above. He or she will enjoy looking, swatting, and grabbing.
- → Let Baby try to grasp a rattle and work it to learn cause and effect.
- → Play "this little piggy" with toes and fingers. Make up something about each digit and end with a good tickle.

6–9 months

- → Play peek-a-boo. Go slow at first so you don't startle Baby. Also hide a toy under a burp cloth and see if they can find it.
- → Blow bubbles toward Baby while strapped in a seat or high-chair. Show them how to pop the bubbles.
- → Place a toy just out of reach and encourage Baby to get to it.
- → Sit with Baby in your lap and play row-row-row-your-boat. Watch out for the stormy seas!

9–12 months

- → Roll a ball or toy car back and forth to each other.
- → Place some blankets over some chairs. Play follow the leader or chase through the tunnels.
- → Play "advanced" find it by placing a toy under a few layers of burp cloths or cups.
- → Play stack it and knock it with soft blocks, cups, or bowls. Simple puzzles are great fun as well.
- → Have Baby mimic what you do. Stick out your tongue, pat your tummy, clap, hide your eyes, and laugh.

How to Read to a Baby

It's never too early to start reading to your child. The American Academy of Pediatrics recommends you begin reading aloud daily to your baby at six months of age. Some parents start much earlier. The more words your baby hears the better it is for growth and development. Reading is also a great bonding opportunity for Dad. And Baby gets to experience three of their favorite things with reading: seeing you, hearing you, and being held by you.

During the first six months, don't expect too much reaction or focus. Use reading as a change of pace and as a fun activity. Around six months of age your baby will start to show more interest. At this age through the first birthday, your baby may hammer at the pages as they learn about turning. They may also focus more, mimic your sounds (moo), show preferences in books, and of course chew on the books.

How To

→ Choose sturdy books that can survive early interaction with Baby. Board books with their heavy-duty pages are a good choice.

→ Choose books with pictures and bright colors. Books with flaps to open are always fun.

→ Find out what your favorite books were as a child and buy some of those. It will be fun to take the nostalgia full circle.

→ Hold your baby while you read.

→ Use all your best voices, noises, and facial expressions to make the reading fun.

→ Grab a minute or two or ten to read as Baby allows. Once they lose interest, stop. Don't force it.

→ Don't try to teach letters and sounds in the first year. Just have fun.

→| Have fun choosing books. Here is a list of ten classics and newer titles that would be a great start to your library:

- *The Very Hungry Caterpillar* by Eric Carle
- *Good Night Moon* by Margaret Wise Brown
- *The Little Engine That Could* by Watty Piper
- *Guess How Much I Love You* by Sam McBratney
- *Sheep in a Jeep* by Nancy Shaw
- *Corduroy* by Don Freeman
- *Where's the Poop* by Julie Markes
- *Baby Animal Friends* by Phoebe Dunn
- *Spot* book series by Eric Hill
- *Goodnight Gorilla* by Peggy Rathman

NOTES

How to Survive Teething

Usually around five to seven months of age a baby's first tooth will appear. The typical batting order of tooth eruption is the two front teeth on the bottom, followed by the four front teeth on top, followed by two more adjoining front teeth on the bottom. Most children will have all twenty of their primary (baby) teeth by age three.

The road to getting those teeth can be painful for the child and the parents. Classic teething symptoms include fussiness, waking during normal sleep, chewing on things (including their hands), and drooling. Every baby is different and may show other symptoms. Every baby also has different tolerance levels. If you suspect your baby is teething, consult with your pediatrician and follow the guidance. Below are some tips on how to get your little one some relief when it is confirmed your baby is teething.

How To

→ Wipe Baby's face and neck often to remove drool. If you have a drool fountain going, you may want to keep an absorbent bib on Baby.

→ Massage Baby's gums with your clean fingers.

→ Give Baby something cool (cold) to chew on. Teething rings are great as is a wet washcloth placed in the freezer for about thirty minutes.

→ Remember to clean teething rings, washcloths, and bibs after each use.

→ Try cold food such as applesauce or peaches if your little one is eating solids. A baby bottle filled with ice water can also be worth a try.

→ Check with your pediatrician to see if Baby Orajel applied directly to the gums is an option.

- Ask your pediatrician if Infant Tylenol (acetaminophen) is an option if nothing else helps. Your doctor will tell you how much to use and when.
- Remember to see a dentist by your child's first birthday. They can spot any potential problems and advise you on great preventive care.

NOTES

How to Spoon Feed a Baby

At the right age your child's pediatrician will give you the green light on feeding solid foods. Be sure to follow the guidelines for what foods and when. Even when they eat some solid food, your baby will still be getting large quantities of breast milk or formula throughout the first year. As a general rule most babies will start trying solid foods around four to six months. Your baby will need to have some control of their head movements and be able to sit well with support before tackling spoon-feeding.

Most babies start out eating rice cereal mixed with breast milk or formula once a day. On your pediatricians cue you will introduce vegetables, fruits, and other baby foods one at a time and stick to feeding it for three days. This allows time to see if your baby has any allergic reactions. By eight or nine months, your baby will probably be up to three spoon-feeding sessions per day along with a full routine of milk feedings.

How To

→ Gather gear for your feeding session: highchair, rubber tipped feeding spoon, baby food, small feeding dish, and bib. A video camera is a must for the first feeding session.

→ Pick your feeding location. At or near the kitchen table is good. Never feed over carpet or a hard to clean floor. Don't feed in front of the TV.

→ Warm Baby's food if necessary. Your baby will like some food warm and some cooler, just like you do. Vegetables may go better if warm, while fruit may go better cool.

→ Avoid trying to feed when Baby is tired or fussy.

→ Don't feed directly from a baby food jar. Bacteria from Baby's mouth rides back on the spoon and won't allow you to use leftover food in the jar later.

- Keep good eye contact with Baby and encourage him or her.
- Load your spoon from the dish and move it to Baby's mouth. Get as much as possible into Baby's mouth. Elevate spoon handle as you remove it so gravity can help food fall into Baby's mouth.
- Scrape off what came out of the mouth with your spoon and load it in again. Give Baby time to work it and swallow. Load spoon and go again.
- Go with Baby's tempo; don't hurry but don't go to slow. When they are done, you will know.

How to Manage Travel with a Baby

Consider going light on your trips and vacations in Baby's first year, at least in the first few months. Do less now as the big vacations you dream of with your kids will come soon enough. Another good rule of thumb for baby travel is to leave half of every day at your destination free and unscheduled.

Think hard about your end destinations in first year travel. You are now in search of "kid friendly." That barefoot cruise off the coast of Africa probably isn't a good choice—especially when your baby gets that first ear infection. Also think twice about staying with friends who don't have children. The hour-long crying spell at 2:00 a.m. or trying to baby proof their house on the fly might not be fun for anyone.

How To

→ Make a strong list of things to pack. Remember diapers, changing pad, wipes, plastic bags (for dirty diapers), diaper rash cream, hand sanitizer, blankets, pacifiers, medicines, toys, clothes, burp cloths or bibs, milk and food, bottles, and stroller or carry sling.

→ Always keep one change of clothes handy for everyone. This includes during air travel. One vomit bomb in your lap and the whole plane will be glad you have the extra clothes.

→ Take plenty of food or milk. A full extra day's worth is a good idea. If you have a canceled flight or a car break down, you will have some cushion.

→ For car travel take a thermos of warm water to make formula bottles on the fly. If using chilled milk, take a thermos of hot water and a large cup. Fill the cup halfway with the hot water and set bottle inside to warm it.

→ Avoid travel schedules that cut it close on time. A baby slows you down and requires more pit stops. Be patient and take breaks when needed.

→ Try to travel during Baby's naptime, so he or she can sleep for a good chunk of the trip. Some parents even like to travel at night.

→ Remember to take Baby's birth certificate for identification during air travel.

→ Ask the airline prior to your trip how strollers and car seats are handled.

→ Ask the airline what milk/formula/food/bottles can be carried on and if a bottle can be warmed in flight.

→ Take full advantage of family preboarding on flights. You will need the extra time to get settled.

_____

_____

_____

_____

_____

_____

_____

_____

NOTES

How to Choose a Daycare

Choosing a daycare provider that's right for you and your child can be tough. Like other purchasing decisions, the key is to arm yourself with good information and referrals, look at the product first hand and trust your instincts.

Whenever possible both parents should visit the prospective caregivers. Two heads and hearts are always better when it comes to making decisions of this importance. Arm yourself with a list of questions, take notes, and visit more than one place to get some perspective.

How To

→ Get referrals. What do other people you know think about the daycare providers they are using?

→ Decide what facility locations might work. Some will be too far out of the way to be considered.

→ Do the facilities you want to consider have an opening for your child?

→ Google the facility or provider to see what you can find out. Check the Better Business Bureau as well.

→ Narrow it down to a list of finalists to visit.

→ Are there other caregivers you really want to use but they are full? If so, see if you can get on a waiting list for a future slot.

→ Start with these questions and add your own at each place you visit:

- Is the staff energetic, pleasant, and calm? Do employees seem as if they want to be there?
- What is the staff experience in working with children?
- Is the facility licensed if applicable? How long has the facility been in business?

- Does the staff seem genuinely interested in you and your child?
- What is the staff-to-child ratio? What is the maximum number of children the facility will take?
- Is the facility clean, bright, and cheerful? Are appropriate areas baby proofed? Are children in highchairs strapped in? Are diaper changing areas and bathrooms clean and sanitary?
- What are the procedures and times for drop off and pick up?
- What safety and security procedures are in place?
- What are the policies for sick children?
- What would be a typical day's schedule for your child?
- Do you hear and see signs of happy children?
- How do they use TV or videos if at all for your child's age group?
- What is the parent drop in policy?
- Are there written contracts to review and references to call?
- How much do they charge? Do you pay when on vacation? Are there late fees or other regular costs?

NOTES

How to Make a Killer Lasagna

The following recipe is a hearty dish spiced up with a little salsa, and it makes plenty for leftovers as well. It is a great dish to prepare and refrigerate the night before or in the morning before work. The first person home pops it in the oven. Enjoy with a salad.

Here are the ingredients and tools you need to make it happen:

1 pound lean ground beef or chicken (your choice)
1 cup mild or medium picante sauce (your choice)
1 cup tomato paste
½ cup chopped onions
¾ cup water
2 teaspoons dried basil
2 teaspoons dried oregano
1 cup ricotta cheese (can sub cottage cheese if necessary)
2 cups shredded mozzarella cheese
1 box uncooked lasagna noodles
Large skillet, large mixing bowl, mixing spoon, and 7"x11" baking pan

How To

→ Cook beef and onion in skillet until done. If using chicken, cook the pieces and then remove. Chop into small pieces and return to skillet.

→ Add tomato paste, picante sauce, water, basil, and oregano to skillet. Mix well and set aside.

→ Combine ricotta cheese and ¾ cup mozzarella cheese in mixing bowl. Mix well and set aside

→ Coat baking pan with vegetable oil or nonstick spray.

→ Layer baking pan as follows: ½ cup meat sauce, layer of lasagna noodles, and half of cheese mixture.

- Repeat layers: meat sauce, noodles, and remaining cheese mixture.
- Top with remaining sauce and then remaining 1¼ cups of mozzarella cheese.
- Coat inside of a foil cover with vegetable oil or nonstick spray. Cover and refrigerate. Clean up the kitchen.
- When ready, bake in preheated oven at 350° for 1 hour. Remove from oven and let cool for 10 minutes before serving.

_____

_____

_____

_____

_____

_____

_____

_____

_____

_____

NOTES

How to Make
a Classic Chicken Casserole

Every man needs a classic chicken casserole in his toolbox of tricks. This tasty recipe will feed your house for at least a couple of days. It can be made just prior to baking; or you can make it up ahead of time, refrigerate, and bake just before dinner. Grandma would be proud of this one.

Round up the following ingredients and tools to get it done:

3 cups chicken breast (about 1½ pounds)
2 cups chopped celery
¼ cup chopped onion
1 eight-ounce can water chestnuts
2 cans cream of chicken soup
½ cup mayonnaise and ½ cup sour cream
1 tablespoon salt and ¾ teaspoon pepper
2 tablespoons lemon juice
½ cup dried cranberries
1½ cup sliced almonds
3 cups crushed corn flakes or crackers (Ritz, Club, or others)
½ cup melted light or regular butter
Measuring cup, measuring spoons, vegetable oil
Mixing spoon, large mixing bowl, and 9"x13" baking dish.

How To

→ Start frying or boiling your chicken.
→ Chop celery and onion while chicken is cooking.
→ Mix celery and onion in a large mixing bowl with the following: water chestnuts, cream of chicken soup, mayonnaise, sour cream, salt, pepper, lemon juice, cranberries, and 1 cup sliced almonds.

- Take fully cooked chicken and chop it into penny-sized pieces or smaller. Put into bowl with the other ingredients and mix well.
- Take vegetable oil and spread lightly on inside of baking dish.
- Pour mixed ingredients into baking dish and spread evenly.
- Wipe measuring cup and mixing bowl clean.
- Measure out 3 cups of corn flakes or crackers. Place in mixing bowl and crush. Have fun with this!
- Add the remaining ½ cup of sliced almonds.
- Melt ½ cup of butter and add to mixing bowl with cornflakes/crackers and almonds. Mix well.
- Spread this topping mixture evenly over other ingredients in baking dish.
- Cover and refrigerate if baking later. Clean up.
- When ready to bake, cook uncovered at 350° for 1 hour. Cook for an extra 5 minutes if pulling from the refrigerator. Serve and enjoy!

NOTES

How to Make
Gina's Grape Wow

This is a super-tasty dish that is quick and easy. It makes a great side for breakfast, lunch, or dinner. Or you can use it as a snack or desert. This is the stuff heroes are made of. Enjoy.

You need the following ingredients and tools:

      8-ounce sour cream
      8-ounce cream cheese
      ½ cup brown sugar
      ½ cup pecan chips
      1 pound green grapes
      1 pound red seedless grapes
      Large serving bowl and small mixing bowl
      Measuring cup and mixing spoon

How To

→ Rinse grapes well and slice all in half. Put sliced grapes in large bowl.

→ Mix cream cheese and sour cream in small mixing bowl.

→ Stir the cream mixture into grapes in large bowl.

→ Mix brown sugar and pecan chips well in small bowl.

→ Stir half of the sugar/pecan mixture into large bowl with grapes.

→ Level grape mixture, and then layer remaining sugar/pecan mix on top.

→ Cover and refrigerate. Lick spoon well and clean kitchen well.

Sources

1. *Facts for Features, Mothers Day, May 11, 2008*, U.S. Census Bureau, http://www.census.gov/Press-Release/www/releases/archives/facts_for_features_special_editions/011633.html (updated 13 March 2008; accessed 08 August 2008).

2. *Father Facts*, 5th ed. (Gaithersburg, Maryland: National Fatherhood Initiative, 2007).

3. Mark Lino, *Expenditures on Children by Families, 2006*; Miscellaneous Publication No. 1528-2006 (Washington, D.C.: U.S. Department of Agriculture, Center for Nutrition Policy and Promotion, 2007).

4. FinAid, *College Cost Projector*, http://www.finaid.org/calculators/costprojector.phtml (updated 2008; accessed 09 August 2008).

5. Dave Ramsey, "The Seven Baby Steps," http://www.daveramsey.com/etc/cms/index.cfm?intContentID=2867 (updated 2008; accessed 08 August 2008).

6. J. A. Martin and F. Menacker, *Expanded Health Data from the New Birth Certificate, 2004*, National Vital Statistics Reports, vol. 55 no. 12 (Hyattsville, Maryland: National Center for Health Statistics, 2007).

7. *Car Safety Seats: A Guide for Families 2008*, American Academy of Pediatrics, http://www.aap.org/FAMILY/carseatguide.htm (updated 2008; accessed 08 August 2008).

8. *Baby Blues*, American Pregnancy Association, http://www
.americanpregnancy.org/firstyearoflife/babyblues.htm (updated
April 2004; accessed 09 August 2008).

9. *Prevalence of Self-Reported Postpartum Depressive Symptoms—
17 States, 2004–2005,* Centers for Disease Control and Prevention,
http://www.cdc.gov/mmwr/preview/mmwrhtml/mm5714a1.htm
(updated 11 April 2008; accessed 11 August 2008).

10. *Dental Care for Your Baby,* American Academy of Pediatric
Dentistry, http://www.aapd.org/publications/brochures/babycare
.asp (updated 2008; accessed 08 August 2008).

11. Robert Lewis, *About Men's Fraternity*, http://www.mens
fraternity.com/about/about_mens_fraternity.aspx (updated 2008;
accessed 08 August 2008).

Glossary

Absent-mindedness: Condition of forgetfulness that can occur during pregnancy. To overcome, be a helper to your spouse with gentle reminders, lists, and good humor.

Acetaminophen (Tylenol): Over-the-counter pain relief medication. Your wife should get approval from her doctor to take during pregnancy and if nursing. Never give to a child under two years old without clear direction and approval from your pediatrician.

Advice: Words and suggestions often spoken from well-intended friends. Listen carefully, and sift through what you want to use. Can also be directions from a doctor—follow these.

Amniotic fluid: Fluid surrounding Baby in the mother's womb. Also known as the "water" that breaks or will be broken prior to delivery.

Amniocentesis: Process of extracting a sample of amniotic fluid from the mother during pregnancy. Test results provide lots of information about a baby's genetic makeup and overall condition.

Anemia: Condition when pregnant women's blood becomes low on iron or iron-deficient. Often occurs in the third trimester. Can be eliminated with vitamin supplements and a healthy diet. Iron can be found in most fruits, vegetables, grains, and meats.

Anesthesia: Pain relief typically administered during childbirth or other medical procedures. Also see *epidural.*

Antibiotics (the pink medicine): Medicine your child may be prescribed to take for ear infection, illness, or other condition. It can stain your clothes and Baby's clothes as you try to get it down.

APGAR score: Test given to a baby immediately following birth to assess overall health. Each of five criteria is evaluated and scored: appearance or color, pulse or heartbeat, grimace or reflex irritability, activity or muscle tone, and respiration or breathing.

Autism: A birth disorder in which the child fails to develop normal human relationships and interaction. Can vary widely in severity. Often marked by problems in speaking, mannerisms, and behavior.

Baby: Tiny human being who will change your life for the better. Requires you to be present, protect, provide, partner, and play.

Baby Blues: Condition experienced by many new mothers following delivery. Marked by mild depression or anxiety. Typically short term. Dad's job is to listen, encourage, and help. Also see *postpartum depression*.

Baby monitor: Spy gear usually placed in a room with sleeping baby. Allows you to hear and/or see your baby. Also lets you "check on" the baby without entering the room and waking them up.

Baby proofing: Process of making your home a safe place for Baby to explore. Complete the transformation *before* Baby begins to crawl.

Babysitter: Carefully selected and experienced person who will care for your precious baby when both parents are away. Yikes!

Bassinet: Small, lightweight baby bed that can be moved from room to room. Typically used only in the first few months.

Bathing: Fun procedure of gently washing a mostly-clean-anyway baby. Great time to tickle, giggle, make funny faces, and sing favorite 80's hits to your little one.

Bedtime, bedtime routine: Regular lights out time for your little one. Babies (and many adults) like the familiar. Your baby will learn to recognize when it is bedtime by the events leading up to it such as a bath, book, last feeding, low lights, and so forth.

Bed rest: Physician prescribed rest for an expectant mom. Used to minimize the chances of pre-term labor. Not as fun as it sounds, especially after the first day. Encourage and support your wife during this important time.

Bee stings, insect bites: Inconvenient part of nature that must be carefully observed and taken care of on babies. Watch carefully for any allergic reactions, even if both parents are not allergic.

Belly: Container attached to your wife that will be Baby's home during pregnancy. Be sure to touch and admire often.

Belly button: A previously discreet part of the female body that will undergo some dramatic changes during pregnancy. May be the "point of the spear" when people see your expectant wife coming toward them.

Bib: Device feeding baby wears around neck; designed to keep anywhere from 5 to 95 percent of food off of his or her clothes. Usually won't help protect you or your clothes.

Bilirubin: Chemical formed in the blood during the normal breakdown of red blood cells, usually removed from blood by the liver. Newborns livers often don't remove all the bilirubin produced which leads to a yellowish appearance known as newborn jaundice.

Bililights: Fluorescent light that alters bilirubin, making it easier for a new baby's liver to process it. May be administered in the hospital or in some cases at home. Bili-blankets that wrap around the baby are an alternative.

Birth certificate: Important document needed from kindergarten to college; filed with your state's Office of Vital Records. The hospital staff will often initiate this but check to make sure. If giving birth at home you will need to initiate the filing.

Birth control: Any number of methods used to prevent pregnancy including pills, condoms, and others.

Birthing room: Most often found in a hospital setting, this will be the room where your baby is actually delivered. You may move from this room to another for the remainder of your stay.

Birthmarks: Reddish blotches or other colored spots on a newborn, many of which disappear over time. Discuss all the bumps and colors you see with your pediatrician so you know what to expect and so you can explain them to Aunt Marge when she inquires.

Blanket: Device used to wrap or "swaddle" an infant. Your child may become attached to a favorite. Larger version used by adults in an attempt to rest once they become parents.

Bloody show: Pink or blood-streaked vaginal mucus discharge. Usually means labor will start within a day, but may end up being several days. Your wife should always consult with her physician about what she is seeing and feeling.

Books: Tools used for learning and becoming a more effective spouse and parent. Also object to use for entertaining and engaging baby.

Bottle feeding: Procedure of using a baby bottle loaded with formula or breast milk to feed a baby. You may have to experiment with different bottle types and nipples to find a combination you and your baby both like.

Bouncer seat: Miracle invention into which you can strap your baby for a change of pace. May vibrate or play music. Has a slight bounce or spring when the baby moves or when moved by an adult.

Bowel movements: Physician term for "pooping." Babies have all kinds. Will vary in consistency, color, quantity, and odor.

Braxton-Hicks: Not a law or accounting firm but a type of contraction known as false labor. This is the warm-up drill your wife's uterus goes through to get ready for the real game.

Breast-feeding: Artful process your wife may engage to feed your baby. Can become tiring so do all you can to support the process, such as delivering the baby ready to go as well as handling other household and baby chores.

Breech: When Baby is positioned in the womb to come out tail first. Normal and preferred position is headfirst. Depending on stage of pregnancy, Baby may or may not be able to switch.

Brushing teeth: Something you will want to get in the habit of doing for your baby once that first tooth appears. Take your baby to a dentist by their first birthday so you can get proper instruction on how to care for those gems.

Burping: Process of extracting air from Baby's stomach during feeding. And you thought you were the belch king in high school; wait until you hear this little one rip 'em! Refer to Power Module section for the how to.

Bulb pump, bulb syringe: Small device used to clear Baby's nose or mouth. Often used to pull mucus out to help Baby breathe.

Bumpers: Not a part of your car. For babies, these are the nice pads surrounding the inside of their cribs. Helps protect little noggins and other body parts from hitting the hard sides of the bed.

Camera: Device used to record history and capture the most memorable moments of your life. Dude, as a new dad you need to be all over this one.

Carrier (backpack, front pack, sling): Various contraptions you wear and carry a baby in. Designed to comfortably hold the baby, leaving your arms free to do other tasks. Poll your friends with babies to see which ones they like.

Car seat: Mandatory safety seat for transporting your baby in a car. Two of dad's top jobs are to make sure the seat is installed correctly in the car and that baby is installed correctly in the seat.

Catheter: A tube inserted into your wife's bladder to drain urine during delivery. Used if epidural or C-section is in play.

Cereal, rice cereal: Babies first solid food usually given between four and six months. Make sure you get your pediatrician's clearance before administering. Get the camera! Some parents believe this is the miracle drug that helps their baby sleep through the night.

Cervix: The lower part of the uterus (womb). It forms a canal that opens into the vagina, which leads to the outside of the body.

Cesarean section (C-section): Surgical procedure where baby is delivered through an incision in your wife's abdomen rather than vaginally. Discuss with your wife's doctor ahead of time what circumstances might lead to a C-section.

Changing table: Tall, padded table or dresser designed for diaper changing. This is a key purchase or gift. You will be spending lots of time here. If it requires assembly, be double sure you have done it correctly.

Checkups: Broad term for regularly scheduled physician office visits for your pregnant spouse and then for your baby. As a dad you need to be at these appointments and be an active participant. Ask questions, listen, and take notes.

Circumcision: Surgical removal of penis foreskin on male infants. Ouch. Also a decision you and your wife will need to discuss and make if you are having a baby boy.

Cleft lip, cleft palate: A medical condition where parts of the upper lip or palate (roof of the mouth) don't grow together correctly. Can often be largely corrected with surgery, therapy, and dental work.

Clumsiness: Condition that can sometimes accompany pregnancy. Don't just giggle; hold out your hand and be the rock your wife can steady herself on.

Coach: Your title in the delivery room. Your key plays are encouragement, support, advocacy, hand holding, and reminding your wife she can do this. These are the same great plays to use throughout pregnancy.

Colic: Long periods (hours) of screaming and crying on a consistent basis (weeks) where your baby seems inconsolable (nothing works). This one can hurt you. Work closely with your pediatrician and your wife to make it through. Often begins to ease up after about three months of age.

College: The last big-ticket item you can help provide for your baby. The key is to start saving some dollars early on and use time and compound interest to help build a college fund. Give your child opportunity.

Colostrum: If your wife is breast-feeding, this is the first liquid her body produces in the first few days after delivery. Nature gets it right with this stuff—it is the ideal food for your new baby's body and immune system.

Constipation: Bowel condition where the mail doesn't get delivered. Can occur in your wife during pregnancy or after delivery and can occur in babies. Work with your physicians to get the packages moving again.

Costs: A baby will cost you some money and some time. Actually lots of money and lots of time. But know that it is the best investment in the world.

CPR: Cardiopulmonary resuscitation. Dude, now that you are a father, you need to know how to do this life-saving procedure on babies and adults. Check out the training available in your community. Be prepared to save a life.

Crawling: First mode of transportation your baby will develop usually sometime in the first year of life. Parents may also revert to this as they try to get to the coffee pot after a long night with baby.

Crib: Bed designed for babies. Make sure yours is put together correctly. For safety reasons don't use an antique or one more than ten years old. They may not be up to current safety standards.

Crowning: Not a ceremony at the Miss America pageant. This is when your baby's head becomes visible during childbirth. Very cool.

Crying: Language used by babies to communicate their needs to the world and their sleepy parents. Hard to understand at first, but you will eventually learn what each different tone, volume, and nuance means. Adults may also revert to this language on occasion.

Crying it out: Can be the last bridge for some babies to cross as they learn to sleep through the night. Discuss at length with your pediatrician and your wife before you go here.

Cup: Tool your baby will eventually use to transfer liquids into his or her mouth. Also see *sippy cup.*

Date — with your wife: Often forgotten art of spending time one on one outside the house with your soul mate. Key part of keeping your marriage engine running strong. Be a leader in setting up dates.

Day and night confusion: Condition where your baby wants to party all night and then sleep during the day. Remember they have been in the dark for nine months and don't know there is a difference. Fear not, as your little one will gradually make the turn and figure it out.

Daycare: Place where your baby may stay while both parents are working. Choose carefully, and be comfortable with the staff and overall program.

Delivery: Process of Baby moving from your wife's body out into the world. One of the best days of your life. Be there, participate and enjoy.

Dental — pregnancy and baby care: Infection of the gums in pregnancy can lead to premature labor. Make sure your wife visits her dentist at least once during pregnancy and is taking proper care of her teeth and gums. Your new baby should visit a dentist by their first birthday so you can learn what to do.

Depression: A serious mental and emotional "down" state that can follow delivery. Watch closely for the signs and take action to help. Don't be afraid to ask for assistance from your wife's physicians. This condition is usually temporary.

Development: The general progress your baby makes while growing. Know that all babies are on a different track and timetable. Don't be freaked out by what the Jones baby is "already doing" next door. Talk to your doctor if you're concerned.

Diabetes (gestational): One of the most common pregnancy complications and also one of the easiest to manage. Around 28 weeks most physicians check for this with a simple blood test. This is the one where your wife consumes the legendary big orange drink prior to testing.

Diagnostic tests: Along with a traditional ultrasound, you may be offered a number of other tests during pregnancy to assess the health and condition of your child. Discuss the pros and cons of each with your spouse. Also see *amniocentesis.*

Diaper: Device worn by a baby near the waist to keep your house and clothes clean. Typically disposable although may be cloth. Your baby will likely have in excess of 4,000 changes of this device in their life. Strive to change more than your share.

Diaper bag: Combination briefcase, lunchbox, and survival kit for Baby. You won't be leaving the house with Baby without one of these. Even if the design is a little floral and feminine for your taste, know that real men aren't afraid to carry one. It is a badge of honor.

Diaper rash: Redness and rash on Baby's bottom and private area that comes with the territory when wearing diapers. Head it off at the pass with regular diaper changes (get the poop off ASAP) and a good diaper rash ointment.

Diaper wipes: Magical and moist disposable cloths you will use to clean your baby's bottom after a blowout. Also handy for wiping noses and cleaning up lunch time highchair messes.

Dilation of cervix: Opening of the cervix. This is the process where the door opens for the baby to move into the birth canal (vagina) during delivery.

Doctors: Medical professionals who come in a variety of flavors. You need to be involved in the selection of at least two: an OB/GYN for pregnancy and delivery and a pediatrician to care for your new baby.

Doppler: Handheld ultrasound device often used for detecting and amplifying Baby's heartbeat while in the mother's womb. Cool tool.

Doula: A person trained as a labor coach. Can be a welcome addition to hire for your pregnancy and delivery team.

Down Syndrome: A chromosome disorder occurring in some babies. There is no cure.

Dressing: The art of getting a very tiny body with very tiny feet and tiny hands into very tiny clothes. With practice you will become a pro. Refer to the Power Module section for more help.

Dropping (lightening): When the fetus moves down into the pelvic cavity. For first time moms, this usually occurs a few weeks before go time.

DtaP (diphtheria, tetanus, acellular pertussis vaccine): A series of shots given in the first year and beyond to guard against diphtheria, tetanus, and pertussis (whooping cough).

Due date: A ballpark date for when your baby will arrive. Calculated by your wife's physician based on several factors. Unfortunately babies in the womb aren't good at reading calendars, so they typically show up when they want to.

Ear infection: A new parent's enemy caused by the tiny plumbing in babies' ears that may not allow fluid to drain easily. Can be painful and uncomfortable for a baby and result in crying and interrupted sleep for everyone. Usually, it's easy to treat. See also *otitis media.*

Effacement: Term for thinning of the cervix during labor.

Emotions: Feelings. You and your wife will have a full range during pregnancy, delivery, and the baby's first year. You might even find some new ones, especially when you hold your baby for the very first time.

Encouragement: Your wife needs a constant dose of this from you during these crazy new times. Think like a dump truck and heap it on her.

Endometriosis: Medical condition where tissue similar to the lining of the uterus grows elsewhere in the body, usually in the pelvic cavity. It can lead to infertility in some women.

Epidural: Method of delivering anesthesia during childbirth via a large needle inserted near the mother's spine. Helps reduce the pain of delivery. Procedure also keeps many husbands from being physically harmed by their wives during delivery.

Episiotomy: Incision made during delivery to enlarge the vaginal opening. Helps make more room for the head to get through. Discuss the playbook for an episiotomy with her physician ahead of time.

Exercise: Miracle drug to be taken throughout life. Join with and support your wife in regular exercise during pregnancy and following delivery. Always get clearance from her physician for an exercise program.

"ExerSaucer" (stationary entertainer): A fun zone for Baby featuring a variety of rattles, spinners, and toys. Often used later in the first year when Baby is able to hold his or her head up.

Exhaustion: See *fatigue*.

External fetal monitoring: Most often two devices strapped to the mother's abdomen during delivery. One monitors fetal heartbeat, and the other measures the intensity and duration of uterine contractions. You will be able to watch the contractions coming and help your wife get through them.

Eye ointment: An antibiotic ointment applied to a newborn's eyes to prevent certain infections. It is required in most states.

False labor: Not the real deal—but often hard to tell from the real deal. Always talk to your doc about what is going on and if any doubt exists, head to the hospital on their recommendation to be sure.

Family: The key foundational block of society. Should be the number-one priority and first consideration in everything you do.

Family Medical Leave Act (FMLA): Federal law that applies to some companies. Allows you to take up to twelve weeks of unpaid leave during pregnancy and following delivery. Essentially holds a job for you until you return. Dads may be eligible as well.

Family practitioner: All-purpose physician. Depending on the practice, he or she may care for adults, children, and even deliver babies. Or they may be more specialized.

Father and fatherhood: The most prestigious and demanding job you will ever do. Give it all you have got in pregnancy, delivery, and the many years following.

Fatigue: State of being physically or mentally tired or both. Also known as being pooped. Very likely to occur with adults who have a new baby in the house. Do as much as possible to protect you and your wife from this condition.

Feeding: Art of getting food into a baby. May be accomplished with a breast, bottle, baby spoon, or the baby's own hands. If you are involved, don't wear a white shirt.

Fetal Alcohol Syndrome: Caused by heavy alcohol consumption in pregnancy. Produces infants with a host of complications, many of which last a lifetime. Be a leader and a partner and support your wife in an alcohol-free pregnancy.

Fetal movement: Punches, kicks, pokes, turns, and other tricks your baby will perform while riding along in Mom's tummy. Mom gets to feel them all, but make sure she lets you feel some with your hand.

Fetus: Term for a baby in the womb.

Fever (in Baby): Not good. Any fever in a baby under six months old requires an immediate call to your pediatrician. That means immediate—not in the morning. Learn your doctor's guidelines for fever in an older baby as well.

First words: A huge milestone where Baby begins to move verbal communication from just crying to talking and crying. "Da-da," "Ma-ma," "ball," or any other first word is sweet music.

Five P's: Not a cool new band but your marching orders as a husband and new father. The Five P's are: be Present, Protect, Provide, Partner, and Play. Work hard at these and you will be greatly rewarded.

Flowers: Mandatory gift for husband to give wife following childbirth. Ideally presented within a few hours of delivery. Diamonds or other significant gifts may be substituted with discretion. Household appliances and/or cash will not be well received.

Flu shot: Annual vaccination you and your wife should get. Most pregnant women can also get a flu shot, so talk to your physician. Pregnancy + flu = not good. Also ask your pediatrician if your baby is a candidate for a flu shot.

Fluids: Liquids (water being the best) your wife will want to be drinking plenty of while pregnant. Good tool to prevent constipation. Same goes for Baby.

Folic acid: A key vitamin for women to consume prior to conception and during pregnancy. Found in whole grains and leafy, green vegetables. Can help reduce the risk of neural tube defects such as spina bifida.

Fontanels: See soft spot in Baby's head.

Food cravings, food aversions: Condition where your pregnant wife is crazy in love with a particular food or can't stand some others. Stand ready to be her "knight in shining armor" if she needs you to make an ice cream run.

Forceps: Medical instrument similar to salad tongs that may be used to help pull the baby along during delivery. Talk to your physician prior to delivery regarding forceps and circumstances when they might be used.

Formula: Souped-up milk designed for babies. Science is getting this close to breast milk in effectiveness.

Freezer: Household appliance to be used as much as possible. When friends and family ask what they can do to help, mention that meals are appreciated. You and your wife will need all the extra time and energy you can muster, and a full freezer can help. Think mountain man storing up firewood for the winter.

Fussiness: Baby's way of communicating they aren't crazy about their current circumstances. May be marked by fidgeting, crying, or screaming like a siren. May also be present in pregnant women on bed rest.

Gas: Air bubbles that naturally form in a baby's stomach during feeding. Can be painful if not removed with regular burping during feeding. Some bubbles may be passed out the other end. The technical term for this is a fart.

Genetic screening and counseling: Process of testing adults for certain genetic disorders such as cystic fibrosis, sickle-cell anemia, and others. Based on the information a genetic counselor can give the odds of children having the disorder and provide other information.

Glucose screening test: Blood test done at about twenty-eight weeks in pregnancy to check for gestational diabetes. Also known as the "big orange drink" test.

Grandparents: Parents of Baby's parents. Invaluable resource. Consider yourself lucky if you have some who are involved.

Growth charts: Statistical curves that compare your baby's height and weight to others. Main emphasis is to see steady growth over time, not to compete for position.

Gynecologist: See *obstetrician / OB-GYN*.

Hep B (hepatitis B vaccine): A series of shots your baby will receive to guard against Hepatitis B, a chronic liver disease. The

Hepatitis A vaccine may also be recommended once your child is older than the age of two. Consult your pediatrician.

Hemorrhoids: Swollen veins in the rectum. Common problem during pregnancy and following delivery. Follow the physician's advice in prevention and treatment.

Hib (hemophilus influenzae b vaccine): A series of shots given in the first year to protect against hemophilus influenzae b, a bad news bacteria that can cause a number of serious infections in your little one. No relation to the common flu.

High blood pressure: Condition your wife will be checked for throughout pregnancy. Make sure you aren't adding to her stress and pushing those levels up. See also *preeclampsia*.

Highchair: Contraption designed for feeding small humans. Make sure your little one is properly fastened in it. Also, birthplace of some of the biggest messes you will ever clean up in your life.

High-risk pregnancy: Women in this category may have different issues, including a problem pregnancy before, higher age, genetic problem, or a preexisting medical condition.

Home pregnancy test: Anxious instrument used for finding out if "we are" or "we aren't." Seeing this tool is often when you first realize you are going to be a dad and that life is forever changed.

Hormones: Chemical substances produced by the body that control and regulate the activity of cells and organs. Pregnancy and the time following it can produce floods of hormones in women. Be patient and understanding as you ride the waves. Don't tell your wife she is crazy, illogical, or unreasonable.

Hugs: Universal sign of love and affection. Your wife needs extra doses of these from you during pregnancy, delivery, and the years following. These are good for you too. Crank it up.

Humidifier: Machine that puts extra moisture into the air. May be recommended by your pediatrician if your baby has a cold or in other situations. If you run one, make sure you clean it regularly to avoid mold and bacteria growth.

Ibuprofen (Advil): Over-the-counter pain reliever. Always, always check with your physician before taking during pregnancy or before giving to a child younger than two years of age. Always.

Ice chips: Often given to mothers in labor to help keep their mouths from becoming too dry. Find out where the hospital keeps them so you can get more if necessary.

Immunizations: Shots containing important vaccines that protect against some nasty diseases. Be sure your baby is immunized on schedule.

Induction (labor): The process of jump-starting labor before nature kicks in. May be done for a variety of reasons. Talk to your wife's physician early on about when induction will be considered.

Influenza vaccine: See *flu shot.*

Insurance: Financial protection. You need this for your body and your family's bodies (health), your life (life), your ability to earn an income (disability), your stuff (homeowners or renters), and your car (auto) just to name a few. Get covered now, not later.

IPV (inactivated polio vaccine): A series of shots your baby will receive to prevent the polio disease.

Iron: Key mineral in pregnancy. As more blood is made, the need for iron increases. Low levels can lead to iron-deficiency anemia. Help your wife get the iron she needs with fruits, vegetables, grains, meats, and vitamins.

Jaundice: A condition in newborns marked by a yellow appearance. Caused by an immature liver trying to get rid of bilirubin in the blood. Very common and often treated with special fluorescent lights.

Job / jobs: Common tool used to produce an income to support your family. Find the best one you can because babies are cash burning machines. Be very careful not to lose yourself in your job and neglect your many duties at home.

Jogger stroller: Baby stroller with bicycle-like wheels and tires. Better suited to running or unpaved routes than their small hard-wheeled stroller cousins.

Labor: The hard work of birthing a child, thus the term *labor*. Marked by strong and steady contractions.

Lactation: The process of milk production in moms. May also refer to breast-feeding.

La Leche League: A network of local organizations providing support and advice for breast-feeding moms.

Lamaze: One type of childbirth course centered on relaxation, proper breathing, and support from an awesome spouse (that's you, champ).

Latching on: The artful process of connecting a baby's mouth with a mother's breast. Not as easy as you might think.

Late-night feeding: Procedure of feeding a baby when it is very dark outside and everyone is very sleepy. Usually occurs somewhere between 1:00 a.m. and 4:00 a.m. When bottle-feeding, men should strive to do as many of these as possible. Don't worry—they don't go on forever.

Leaking: Term used to describe the uncontrollable loss of fluid in your wife's body. May be amniotic fluid late in pregnancy or breast milk later on.

Love: Key ingredient in marriage and parenting. As a husband and father, you need to be a love factory and put out a bunch of it. Show it, say it, live it.

Manny: Dude version of a nanny. Someone who helps you take care of your kids, usually in your home.

Massage: A great gift for your wife. Especially good for an expectant mom to help ease the stress and strain of pregnancy. Make sure the massage therapist you choose is trained in prenatal massage. A gentle back massage from you may also help during labor.

Maternity clothes: Larger size clothes your wife will cycle through as she grows during pregnancy. Used to be frumpy in the old days but now there are lots of cool options from which to choose.

Meconium: The first bowel movement or two for your new baby. Usually black or green and tar like in consistency. Like any new engine from the factory your new one has to burn the soot out. After this initial cleaning of the pipes, bowel movements will be more normal, though strong and plentiful. Also see *diaper*.

Messy house: Part of the package deal when a baby begins crawling. They like to leave a trail of destruction and chaos. Make sure you have baby-proofed as discussed and then relax a little. Let them explore within reason.

Midwife: A nurse or trained person other than a physician who delivers babies. Often has a focus on the human and emotional aspect of childbirth.

MMR (measles, mumps, rubella vaccine): A series of shots usually given after the first year to prevent measles, mumps, and rubella (German measles).

Money, money, money: What a growing family consumes. Know that your wife and children are worth every penny.

Mood swings: The up and down emotional state that can accompany women during and after pregnancy. Know when to take cover. Again, make sure you are part of the solution and not part of the problem.

Morning sickness: Nausea and vomiting that may occur during the first trimester of pregnancy. Not much fun. Also not a good name as it can strike at any time of the day or night. Work with a physician to help your wife get through.

Mother and motherhood: The most difficult and prestigious job in the world. If you work hard at being a great father, it will help her be a great mother.

Motor skills: The collection of physical skills your baby will master such as holding his or her head up, grasping objects, and others.

Mucous plug: A "cork" that seals off the opening of the uterus. May come out well before delivery.

Murmur — heart: Any unusual noise made by the heart. All murmurs will be carefully diagnosed by your physician to determine if they are harmless or if they warrant further investigation.

Music: Universal relaxation and entertainment tool. Great for Mom, Dad, and Baby. Try piping in some cool tunes to Baby while in the womb to influence musical tastes. When they are sixteen, you won't have much luck.

Nail trimming: Process of trimming very tiny finger and toenails on very tiny hands and feet. Key to prevent your baby from scratching themselves to pieces.

Name: One of the first decisions you get to make as a parent that lasts a lifetime. Enjoy the selection process with your wife.

Nanny: Hired hand who cares for your children in your home. Make sure you and your wife are comfortable with this person. Check references and observe them in action.

Naps: Another word for a good time. Great medicine for adults and new babies. Do your part to make sure your wife gets these as needed during pregnancy and during that first year.

Nesting: Natural phase of pregnancy where the female prepares her home for the arrival of offspring. May occur at any time. Typically involves flurries of cleaning, decorating, and buying things. Male will be involved but may be asked on occasion to get out of the way.

NICU (neonatal intensive care unit): Unit of a hospital specifically designed and staffed for the care of newborns with serious health issues.

Nightlight: Tiny lights placed strategically in the home. Helps you prevent hitting your big toe, creating a loud commotion, and waking a sleeping baby.

Nurturing: The loving, caring, helping, and stimulating you invest in a new human being. It's a job for both parents.

Obstetrician / OB-GYN: Physician trained in female reproduction and childbirth. Your family's new best friend.

Otitis media: Infection of the middle ear mechanism common in young children. Also see *ear infection.*

Overdue: General term for when a baby hasn't arrived by the calculated date. Discuss strategy with the physician. And be patient—that baby will arrive.

Pacifier: An artificial nipple. Often becomes a comfort and security object for Baby. Can be a great friend if you decide to use it, but it can also be a tough habit for Baby (and you) to break.

Parenthood: Some of the most exciting and educational chapters of life. Involves bringing new human beings into the world and preparing them to prosper on their own. Work hard at it.

Patience: Trait you will need a boatload of during pregnancy, delivery, and the first year.

PCV7 (pneumococcal conjugate vaccine): Helps defend against pneumonia, ear infections, meningitis, blood infections, and some other illnesses. Typically given in a series over the first year.

Pediatrician: Physician trained in the care of kids. Be involved when choosing one to care for yours.

Pitocin (oxytocin): Drug used to induce labor or help spur it along.

Placenta: A temporary organ joining Mom and Baby during pregnancy. It transfers oxygen and nutrients into Baby from Mom and hauls out carbon dioxide and waste produced from Baby. The placenta is expelled after the baby is born.

Playpens (pack and play): A portable bedroom and containment area (jail) for your baby. Make sure you follow the instructions—yes read the instructions—when you set it up. These can be unsafe if you don't do it correctly.

Playgroups: Collection of parents and children who get together on a regular basis for interaction.

Poison control: Process of protecting your child from swallowing something very harmful. Scour your home to the max to be certain anything potentially harmful is locked up or put away where your explorer can't get at it. Also, a call center that can help if your baby does get into something. Call 1-800-222-1222.

Postpartum: The weeks and months following delivery of a baby.

Postpartum depression: Serious condition in new mothers following delivery. Often marked by noticeable emotional and physical issues. Seek treatment with a physician as soon as possible. Help your wife get the help she needs as this is one of the most treatable forms of depression.

Praise: What you need to give to your wife. Tell her she is doing a great job in every phase of pregnancy, delivery, and beyond. She needs to *hear* it even if you think she knows it. So say it out loud regularly. The turbo charged version is praising her in front of other people and her parents.

Praying: Talking in your own way to God. Make sure you are taking a leadership role in your home regarding prayer. Pray with your wife. Pray for your marriage and your children. Pray a lot.

Preeclampsia: Condition in pregnancy marked by high blood pressure. Needs to be treated by a physician. Also known as toxemia.

Pregnancy: Amazing time when another human being grows inside a woman. Also a time when you need to fully engage and start getting things done.

Premature baby: Child born before the thirty-seventh week of pregnancy. Depending on the baby's age and condition at delivery, additional hospital care may be needed.

Prenatal visits: Doctor appointments and checkups that occur during pregnancy. Remember, Dad makes it a priority to go to these too.

Presentation: How the baby is positioning its body in the final weeks before launch (birth). A headfirst presentation is most desirable. A breech presentation means the baby's bottom or feet are trying to arrive first.

Prince Charming: That is you man. Work hard at it.

Pulling up: When your little explorer grabs onto something to help pull from a sitting or crawling position to standing.

Puppy: Cute little pet requiring lots of time, energy, and money. Avoid getting a new puppy and a new baby in the same year if at all possible!

Pushing: The big work in delivery. Your wife will direct all of her strength and attention to pushing at just the right time. You need to be beside her encouraging, coaching, counting, and loving.

Recipe: Assembly instructions for food. Find a few you and your wife like, and then bring them to life on a regular basis. Make enough for leftovers.

Reflexes in newborns: Natural reactions your baby will have to certain things. Examples include startle reflex, sucking reflex (for feeding), and the walking reflex. A favorite for dads is the grasping reflex. Touch the palm of your baby's hand with your finger, and he or she will instinctively grab and squeeze it tight.

Rest: Miracle drug during pregnancy and after Baby arrives. See to it you and your wife have opportunities to rest. May include sleep, sitting, vegging, reading, or other "off duty" time.

Seat belts: Mandatory safety device for all. Be a leader and make sure the car doesn't move until everyone is properly secured.

Shortness of breath: Often occurs during pregnancy due to hormones and a growing baby pushing things around. Severe shortness of breath is not normal and should be treated immediately.

SIDS (Sudden Infant Death Syndrome): The unexpected death of a typically healthy infant. You can help prevent SIDS by putting babies to sleep on their backs, not smoking in the home, using a firm mattress with no loose bedding, and making sure your baby is not dressed too warmly.

Sippy cup: A no spill training cup designed for babies.

Sitting up: Baby skill of moving from crawling or laying down position to sitting without support.

Sitz baths: Warm bath used to relieve discomfort in the rectal and vaginal areas. Especially helpful in the days after childbirth. Also not a good time for you to join her in the tub.

Sleep: Toughest commodity to find with young children in the house. Work out a plan with your wife to get through the hard times and make sure you are sharing the load.

Smile: The melt-your-heart tool babies use on you. Make sure you smile back. Work hard to also help your wife smile a lot during pregnancy, delivery, and the years beyond.

Smoking: A big no-no for all during pregnancy and with children in the home. Do all you can to help everyone in the family kick the habit. You are going to need the money and extra years quitting adds to your life.

Soft spots in Baby's head: Also called fontanels. Openings in a newborn's skull where the bones haven't grown together yet. Key design feature that allows heads to shape and fit through the birth canal. Also allows for rapid brain growth.

Solids: Food other than milk and other liquids.

Spina bifida: A deformity of the spinal column in a baby. Studies show that chances of this defect are greatly reduced when the mother takes prenatal vitamins with folic acid before and during pregnancy.

Spitting up: Wonderful custom babies have of returning a portion of their meal back to you. Think of it as a tip for your hard work. Often lands on your favorite shirt.

Spotting: Slight bleeding in the vaginal area. Your wife should talk to her physician about any spotting she might be having.

Station (of Baby's head): System for measuring how far the baby's head has progressed through the pelvis. Measured in centimeters from around −5 through 0 to +5 (crowning).

Stool softener: Not a chair cushion. This is one thing your wife may take to help ease her bowels back into good working order after traumatizing them in childbirth.

Stork bites: A certain type of birthmark appearing on the face or neck. They usually fade away in the first couple of years. Talk to your pediatrician about any birthmarks on your baby, and know what to expect and watch for in each.

Stress: Mental strain often occurring when a large load of challenging circumstances present themselves. Manage your own levels and help your wife manage hers. Again, be part of the solution and not part of the problem.

Stroller: Baby's first ride. Do your research and help pick one out that is easy to transport and meets your needs.

Swaddling: Wrapping your little one with a blanket like a burrito. Helps them feel snug and secure. Hold the guacamole and onions. See How-to Power Module section for more details.

Swelling: Any sudden or severe onset of swelling in your wife deserves a call to the doctor. Some swelling in the feet and ankles is very normal. Help her by making sure she gets plenty of breaks off her feet. Also encourage her to drink plenty of water, which oddly enough helps avoid excess water retention.

Teething: Process in Baby's first year and beyond where new teeth grow and push through the gums. Can be painful for all and cost everyone some sleep. Work with your pediatrician to manage the situation as best as possible.

Tests: Medical procedures for gathering information. Your pregnant wife and your new baby will go through a bunch. You should be aware of what each is for and know what the results are.

Thrush: A funky white fungus that can show up in a baby's mouth. When wiped away it exposes a raw red area. Consult with your pediatrician if you suspect the funky fungus has found a home in your little one. It is easily treated.

Time: Precious life commodity that can fly by. Make sure you are giving your family plenty of yours. Don't spend it all at work.

Toddler: Term used to describe a transition period for your baby usually in year two and three. Marked by all kinds of cool stuff like running, falling down, food likes and dislikes, temper tantrums, favorite toys, routines, and other crazy stuff. Similar high maintenance behaviors can be found in some adults.

Toxemia: Condition in pregnancy marked by high blood pressure. Needs to be treated by a physician. Also known as pre-eclampsia.

Toys: Fun objects that consume attention. Examples for children include balls, dolls, and building blocks. Examples for adults include surround sound, golf clubs, and cool cars. Dads often need to surrender the time and money they devote to some toys and invest it back into their marriage and family.

Triplets: Three babies in one pregnancy. That's a deal!

Tubal pregnancy: A pregnancy that takes hold outside the uterus, usually in the fallopian tubes. Medical attention is required. Also called ectopic pregnancy.

Tubes for ears: Surgical insertion of tiny tubes in tiny ears. Helps reduce fluid buildup in the child's ear and prevent further ear infections. Usually a last resort after other treatments such as antibiotics have been tried.

Twins: Double whammy.

Ultrasound: Medical procedure where high frequency sound waves are used to give you the first visual of Baby in Mother's womb. Typically performed once or twice during pregnancy to check Baby's health and development. Though black and white and grainy, you should come away from this procedure with the very first photo of your baby. Clear the refrigerator door; there's a new kid in town.

Umbilical Cord: Baby's lifeline while in the uterus. This is the pipe Mom uses to give blood and oxygen to Baby. At birth many fathers are given the opportunity to cut the cord. Let the attending team know you want to. It is a special dad moment.

Urination: Pregnant women and babies do this a lot. If she says pull over, then do it. There isn't much extra capacity and it isn't good for her to hold it.

Uterus: Magical female body part that houses the baby during pregnancy. Also known as the womb.

Urinary tract infection (UTI): An infection of the pee plumbing. Fairly common for women during pregnancy and can also occur in babies. All cases need to be treated promptly.

Vaccine: See *immunization.*

Vacuum extraction: Medical instrument with a plastic cup that attaches to Baby's head during delivery. Helps physician pull Baby through birth canal. Discuss with your physician prior to delivery when the vacuum play would be called.

Vagina: Another amazing female body part. Also known as the birth canal during delivery.

Vaginal delivery: A birth where the baby passes through the vagina (birth canal) into the world. The majority of babies born arrive via this route. A C-section is the only other way out.

Var (Varicella vaccine): A shot to defend against chicken pox. Usually given after the first year.

Varicose veins: Uncomfortable condition where blood pools in veins, most often in the legs, and causes them to bulge. Make sure your wife works with her physician on ways to prevent and minimize varicose veins.

Vasectomy (snipped): Minor surgical procedure to sterilize males. Involves disconnecting certain male plumbing. Don't complain too much to your wife about the pain, or she will remind you of the much larger pain of childbirth.

Vitamins: Key supplement for women to take prior to conception and during pregnancy. Helps ensure her body and baby get everything they need.

Vomiting: Involuntary exercise of voiding the stomach's contents. Can occur in the early stages of pregnancy. Be a comfort and help if it happens. Also known as barfing, hurling, puking, upchucking, and other colorful terms.

Walkers: A seat inside four wheeled legs that lets Baby rove around the house. Even if you had one of these as a child, they are no longer recommended because of the severe number of injuries that occur. Stationary walkers, also known as "exersaucers," don't move and are a good option with proper supervision.

Walking: Huge baby milestone. Those first steps are a moment to savor. They will be followed by millions more.

Water breaking: See *amniotic fluid.*

Wipes: See *diaper wipes.*

Witch hazel pads: Treatment for soothing hemorrhoids and rectal discomfort during and after pregnancy.

Notes

NOTES

NOTES

NOTES

NOTES

NOTES

NOTES

NOTES

NOTES

NOTES

NOTES

Index

LaVergne, TN USA
05 May 2010
181499LV00004B/194/P